IMPACT ON ISSUES 2016-2018
A Guide to Public Policy Positions
League of Women Voters® of the United States

FOREWARD

Impact on Issues is designed to help League leaders use LWVUS public policy positions effectively at the state and local levels.

In addition to the official statements of position for each program area, this guide briefly traces significant past actions and achievements and indicates links among positions. The LWVUS public policy positions "in brief" listed on pages 1-4 reflect the program adopted by the 2016 Convention of the League of Women Voters of the United States. This listing summarizes the official full statements of position, **which are presented in bold type in the relevant sections of this guide**.

Impact on Issues is an indispensable resource for League leaders. A clear understanding of LWVUS positions, how they interrelate and how they can complement and reinforce state, local and Inter-League Organization (ILO) positions will strengthen the League's "Impact on Issues" at all levels of government.

In applying LWVUS positions to state, local and regional issues, it is the responsibility of the appropriate League board, depending on the level of action, to determine whether member understanding and agreement exists and whether the action makes sense in terms of timing, need and effectiveness. Please refer to "Legislative Action: Working Together to Influence Public Policy" starting on page 1 for tools and procedures for an effective action partnership among the national, state and local levels of the League.

SUMMARY OF PUBLIC POLICY POSITIONS
League of Women Voters® of the United States

REPRESENTATIVE GOVERNMENT

Promote an open governmental system that is representative, accountable and responsive (page 8).

Voting Rights

Citizen's Right to Vote - Protect the right of all citizens to vote; encourage all citizens to vote (page 11).

DC Self-Government and Full Voting Representation - Secure for the citizens of the District of Columbia the rights of self-government and full voting representation in both houses of Congress (page 17).

Election Process

Apportionment - Support apportionment of congressional districts and elected legislative bodies at all levels of government based substantially on population (page 19).

Redistricting - Support redistricting processes and enforceable standards that promote fair and effective representation at all levels of government with maximum opportunity for public participation (page 20).

Money in Politics - Campaign finance regulation should enhance political equality for all citizens, ensure transparency, protect representative democracy from distortion by big money, and combat corruption and undue influence in government. The League believes that campaign spending must be restricted but not banned. The League supports public financing, full disclosure, abolishing SuperPACs and creating an effective enforcement agency (page 22).

Selection of the President - Promote the election of the President and Vice-President by direct-popular-vote. Support uniform national voting qualifications and procedures for presidential elections. Support efforts to provide voters with sufficient information about candidates (page 27).

Citizen Rights

Citizen's Right to Know/Citizen Participation - Protect the citizen's right to know and facilitate citizen participation in government decision-making (page 28).

Individual Liberties - Oppose major threats to basic constitutional rights (page 30).

Constitutional Amendment Proposals - In addition to League positions, consideration should be given to whether a proposal addresses matters of abiding importance, makes our political system more democratic or protects individual rights, could be achieved by less difficult legislative or political approaches, and is more suited to a constitutional and general approach than to a statutory and detailed approach (page 31).

Constitutional Conventions - Concerned that there are many unresolved questions about a Constitutional Convention. Certain conditions must be in place: limited to a single specific topic, full transparency, delegates selected by population, and voting by delegates not by state (page 32).

Public Policy on Reproductive Choices - Protect the constitutional right of privacy of the individual to make reproductive choices (page 32).

Congress and the Presidency

Congress - Support responsive legislative processes characterized by accountability, representativeness, decision making capability and effective performance (page 35).

The Presidency - Promote a dynamic balance of power between the executive and legislative branches within the framework set by the Constitution (page 36).

Privatization

Ensure transparency, accountability, positive community impact and preservation of the common good when considering the transfer of governmental services, assets and/or functions to the private sector (page 37).

INTERNATIONAL RELATIONS

Promote peace in an interdependent world by working cooperatively with other nations and strengthening international organizations (page 40).

United Nations

Support a strong, effective United Nations to promote international peace and security and to address the social, economic and humanitarian needs of all people (page 40).

Trade

Support U.S. trade policies that reduce trade barriers, expand international trade and advance the achievement of humanitarian, environmental and social goals (page 44).

U.S. Relations with Developing Countries

Promote U.S. policies that meet long-term social and economic needs of developing countries (page 46).

Arms Control

Reduce the risk of war through support of arms control measures (page 50).

Military Policy and Defense Spending

Work to limit reliance on military force. Examine defense spending in the context of total national needs (page 52).

NATURAL RESOURCES

Promote an environment beneficial to life through the protection and wise management of natural resources in the public interest (page 55).

Natural Resources

Promote the management of natural resources as interrelated parts of life-supporting ecosystems (page 55).

Resource Management

Promote resource conservation, stewardship and long-range planning, with the responsibility for managing natural resources shared by all levels of government (page 56).

Environmental Protection and Pollution Control

Preserve the physical, chemical and biological integrity of the ecosystem with maximum protection of public health and the environment (page 58).

Air Quality - Promote measures to reduce pollution from mobile and stationary sources (page 64).

Energy - Support environmentally sound policies that reduce energy growth rates, emphasize energy conservation and encourage the use of renewable resources (page 64).

Land Use - Promote policies that manage land as a finite resource and that incorporate principles of stewardship (page 64).

Water Resources - Support measures to reduce pollution in order to protect surface water, groundwater and drinking water (page 65).

Waste Management - Promote policies that reduce the generation and promote the reuse and recycling of solid and hazardous wastes (page 65).

Nuclear Issues - Promote the maximum protection of public health and safety and the environment (page 66).

Public Participation

Promote public understanding and participation in decision making as essential elements of responsible and responsive management of our natural resources (page 68).

Agriculture Policy

Promote adequate supplies of food and fiber at reasonable prices to consumers and support economically viable farms, environmentally sound farm practices and increased reliance on the free market (page 70).

Federal Agriculture Policies - Provide financial support to subsidize agriculture in specific instances, enforce federal antitrust laws to ensure competitive agricultural markets and apply clean air and water regulations to all animal and aquaculture production. The federal government should fund basic agricultural research to provide adequate safety of our food supply (page 70).

SOCIAL POLICY
Secure equal rights and equal opportunity for all. Promote social and economic justice and the health and safety of all Americans (page 73).

Equality of Opportunity

Education, Employment and Housing - Support equal access to education, employment and housing (page 74).

Equal Rights - Support ratification of the Equal Rights Amendment and efforts to bring laws into compliance with the goals of the ERA (page 77).

Federal Role in Public Education
Support federal policies that provide an equitable, quality public education for all children pre-K through grade 12 (page 81).

Fiscal Policy

Tax Policy - Support adequate and flexible funding of federal government programs through an equitable tax system that is progressive overall and that relies primarily on a broad-based income tax (page 82).

Federal Deficit - Promote responsible deficit policies (page 82).

Funding of Entitlements - Support a federal role in providing mandatory, universal, old-age, survivors, disability and health insurance (page 82).

Health Care
Promote a health care system for the United States that provides access to a basic level of quality care for all U.S. residents, including behavioral health, and controls health care costs (page 85).

Immigration
Promote reunification of immediate families; meet the economic, business and employment needs of the United States; be responsive to those facing political persecution or humanitarian crises; and provide for student visas. Ensure fair treatment under the law for all persons. In transition to a reformed system, support provisions for unauthorized immigrants already in the country to earn legal status (page 89).

Meeting Basic Human Needs
Support programs and policies to prevent or reduce poverty and to promote self-sufficiency for individuals and families (page 90).

Income Assistance - Support income assistance programs, based on need, that provide decent, adequate standards for food, clothing and shelter (page 90).

Support Services - Provide essential support services (page 90).

Housing Supply - Support policies to provide a decent home and a suitable living environment for every American family (page 91).

Child Care
Support programs and policies to expand the supply of affordable, quality child care for all who need it (page 94).

Early Intervention for Children at Risk
Support policies and programs that promote the well-being, development and safety of all children (page 95).

Violence Prevention
Support violence prevention programs in communities (page 95).

Gun Control

Protect the health and safety of citizens through limiting the accessibility and regulating the ownership of handguns and semi-automatic weapons. Support regulation of firearms for consumer safety (page 96).

Urban Policy

Promote the economic health of cities and improve the quality of urban life (page 97).

Death Penalty

The LWVUS supports abolition of the death penalty (page 98).

Sentencing Policy

The LWVUS believes alternatives to imprisonment should be explored and utilized, taking into consideration the circumstances and nature of the crime. The LWVUS opposes mandatory minimum sentences for drug offenses (page 99).

Human Trafficking

Oppose all forms of domestic and international human trafficking of adults and children, including sex trafficking and labor trafficking (page 99).

PRINCIPLES

Whatever the issue, the League believes that efficient and economical government requires competent personnel, the clear assignment of responsibilities, adequate financing, coordination among levels of government, effective enforcement and well defined channels for citizen input and review (page 101).

LEGISLATIVE ACTION
Working Together to Influence Public Policy

Effective congressional lobbying on national legislative issues depends on a partnership at all League levels—lobbying in Washington and constituent lobbying at home. The Advocacy Department leads the organization's federal lobbying work and provides information to state and local Leagues about advocacy priorities.

This department, working at the direction of the LWVUS Board, is responsible for developing and implementing strategies for lobbying on national issues and advancing LWVUS program priorities. In Washington, the LWVUS president testifies on Capitol Hill and, with members of the Board, lobbies members of Congress (MCs) through phone calls and office visits. Day-to-day lobbying of MCs, staff members and committees is carried out by the LWV's professional staff lobbyists.

The LWVUS volunteer Lobby Corps (LC) of some 20 Washington-area League members lobbies each month when Congress is in session. Each Lobby Corps member is assigned specific state congressional delegations. Contact the LC chair through the national office for the name of the LC member assigned to your delegation.

While it is the job of the LWVUS Board to take the lead in national action and to keep League action synchronized with the U.S. Congress, national legislation is every League's and every member's business. Each state and local League president is expected to take whatever official action is requested in response to a national Action Alert.

Encourage your members and Board members to contact their legislators on key League national issues because their action greatly enhances the League's clout. It is important to remember, though, that **only a League spokesperson, usually the president, speaks in the name of the League.** Leagues and League members should only lobby their own legislators. Individual members can take action on their own behalf.

Lobbying in Washington is vitally important, but direct lobbying of MCs by constituents often is the key to persuading them to vote the League position. The arguments that League leaders and members make to their representatives or senators can make the difference in how they vote. MCs return to their states or districts regularly during congressional recesses. This is a good time to schedule meetings with them or to talk with them at public events. Please inform your state League and the LWVUS Advocacy Department of your lobbying efforts, along with any important information uncovered during your lobby visit or call (reports may be sent to advocacy@lwv.org).

The LWVUS Grassroots Lobby Corps provides another good way for Leagues to keep in contact with their members of Congress. This online network of activists gets the League message to Congress in a highly effective way. Members of the network receive email action alerts from the LWVUS and then respond by sending quick, targeted, and sometimes last-minute, messages to members of Congress on priority issues before key votes. League members are automatically enrolled in the Grassroots Lobby Corps.

The LWVUS grassroots lobbyists act as liaison between LWV lobbyists on Capitol Hill and local and state Leagues. The grassroots lobbyists work with LWV leaders and activists in targeted states and congressional districts to help develop and implement grassroots lobbying strategies. Call the LWVUS if you want to talk about lobbying strategies or have questions about LWVUS issues, and call if you would like written materials or want to schedule training on grassroots strategies or on getting press coverage.

The LWVUS may call League presidents before critical votes in Congress or when in-depth and ongoing grassroots lobbying is needed from your area. LWV presidents also will receive sample op-ed pieces and letters to the editor on issues on which we are actively lobbying.

League communications on priority legislative issues include:

Action Alerts - Members of the Grassroots Lobby Corps and local and state League presidents receive alerts by email at critical times in the legislative process. An alert not only asks Leagues and League members to take action on a key issue, but also provides substantive and political background information. A quick and easy system for sending an email directly to MCs also is provided.

Each state and local League is expected to take whatever official action is requested in response to a national Action Alert. A League Board may choose not to respond to a particular call to action, but may not take action in opposition to a position articulated by the LWVUS on federal or national issues, or by the state League on state issues. Individual League members of course are always free to take action on whatever they choose as long as they do so in their own name and leave no impression that they speak for the League.

Legislative Action Center on the Web - Current Action Alerts, Legislative Updates and other advocacy tools are posted on the LWVUS website at www.lwv.org.

The LWVUS Board annually adopts a set of advocacy priorities to guide its advocacy work in Congress. The goals are:

- Enhance the League's effectiveness by concentrating resources on priority issues
- Build the League's credibility and visibility by projecting a focused and consistent image
- Ensure that the League has sufficient issue and political expertise to act knowledgeably
- Enable the League to manage resources effectively.

In setting legislative priorities, the Board considers the following:

- Opportunities for the League to make an impact
- Program decisions made at Convention or Council
- Member interest
- Resources available to manage effectively.

The LWVUS Board regularly reviews the legislative priorities and is prepared to make adjustments should new opportunities for effective action emerge. In even numbered years, the LWVUS reviews its current program and positions through the program planning process. Convention delegates then vote on program content for the next biennium.

The LWVUS Bylaws provide that Leagues may act on national program only in conformity with positions taken by the LWVUS. State Leagues are responsible for determining action policies and strategies on state issues and ensuring that the League's message is consistent throughout the state. The LWVUS is responsible for a consistent national message. This helps ensure that the League speaks with one voice and is essential for our effectiveness as an advocacy organization.

Requests from State/Local Leagues for Permission to Act at the Federal Level - All action at the federal level must be authorized by the LWVUS board. This includes any effort aimed at influencing a decision on a federal issue, such as communicating with an elected or appointed official, joining a coalition, taking part in a press conference or rally, or writing a letter-to-the-editor. A state or local League wishing to work in this way on a federal issue or at the national level must consult with the LWVUS about the intended action.

As part of this consultation process, the state/local League is asked to provide the following information in writing:

- The proposed action and the message to be conveyed
- The LWVUS position on which the action is based
- Evidence that the issue is a priority for that state or local League.

Leagues are asked to provide this information on the Federal Action Request Form, which can be found on the LWVUS League Management Site forum.lwv.org.

If a local League is requesting permission to contact its U.S. Senator(s) on an issue that has not been the subject of an LWVUS Action Alert, it should also provide evidence that the action has been authorized by its state League. Appropriate LWVUS Board and staff will review the action request to determine that it is consistent with League positions and that it will not interfere with LWVUS action on a priority issue.

REPRESENTATIVE GOVERNMENT
Promote an open governmental system that is representative, accountable and responsive.

Founded by the activists who secured voting rights for women, the League has always worked to promote the values and processes of representative government. Protecting and enhancing voting rights for all Americans, assuring opportunities for citizen participation, working for open, accountable, representative and responsive government at every level—all reflect the deeply held convictions of the League of Women Voters.

In the 1950s, the League worked courageously to protect fundamental citizen rights and individual liberties against the threats of the McCarthy era. In the 1960s, attention turned to securing "one person, one vote" through apportionment of legislative districts based substantially on population. In the 1970s, members worked to reform the legislative process and open it to citizen scrutiny, and to balance congressional and presidential powers. The League also sought to reform the campaign finance system to reduce the dominance of special interests, affirmed support for the direct election of the President and fought for full voting rights in Congress for the citizens of the District of Columbia.

In the 1980s and 1990s, the League worked to break down the barriers to voting, first through reauthorization of the Voting Rights Act and then through a campaign for passage and implementation of the landmark National Voter Registration Act. Campaign finance reform, with a focus on public financing and on closing loopholes, again was a major activity at the federal and state levels, with the goal of enhancing the role of citizens in the election and legislative processes. In the late 1990s, the fight for DC voting rights was reinvigorated.

During that same period, the League worked to ensure the constitutional right of privacy of the individual to make reproductive choices and opposed term limits for legislative offices.

In the mid- to late 1990s, the League launched its Making Democracy Work campaign, focusing on five key indicators of a healthy democracy: voter participation, campaign finance reform, diversity of representation, civic education and knowledge, and civic participation. The 1998 Convention added "full congressional voting representation for the District of Columbia" to the campaign. State and local Leagues measured the health of democracy in their communities, reported the results and worked with other groups to seek change. The LWVUS report "Charting the Health of American Democracy" took a nationwide measure and made recommendations for change.

In the 2000s, this campaign continued. Convention 2002 decided to update the position on the Selection of the President, focusing not only on the electoral process but on the other factors that affect the presidential race, e.g., money, parties and the media. The position was expanded and formally approved at Convention 2004.

In the second half of the 2000s, the League supported legislation to reform the lobbying process and to rebuild public confidence in Congress. In 2008, the House passed new ethics procedures, including new ethics rules, disclosure requirements for campaign contributions "bundled" by lobbyists, and a new ethics enforcement process. The League also continued its work seeking full enforcement of the National Voter Registration Act.

In late 2010 and again in 2012, the League and coalition partners urged the Speaker to preserve and strengthen House ethics rules and standards of conduct.

Campaign Finance in the 2000s - The five-year fight for campaign finance reform paid off in March 2002 when the President signed the Bipartisan Campaign Reform Act into law. The League was instrumental in developing this legislation and pushing it to enactment, and remains vigilant in ensuring the law is enforced and properly interpreted in the Courts.

In the late 2000s, the LWVUS was involved as a "friend of the court" in two pivotal U.S. Supreme Court cases: *Caperton v. Massey* and *Citizens United v. FEC*. In the latter case, the League argued that corporate spending in elections should not be equated with the First Amendment rights of individual citizens.

In 2010, the League reacted swiftly and strongly to the Supreme Court's adverse decision in the *Citizens United* case, which allowed unlimited "independent" corporate spending in candidate elections. The League president testified before the relevant House committee on the key steps that can be taken to respond, focusing on the importance of including tighter disclosure requirements. The League continues to urge passage of the DISCLOSE Act to ensure that corporate and union spending in elections is fully disclosed.

With the explosion of supposedly "independent" spending by outside groups in the years since *Citizens United*, the League is pushing for tougher rules on coordination, since much of the outside spending is not independent and instead is coordinated with candidate campaigns. In addition, the League continues to push for legislation to protect and reinvigorate the presidential public financing system and to institute congressional public financing as well. The League also is working to reform the dysfunctional Federal Election Commission (FEC), which has refused to enforce the law.

Election Administration in the 2000s - When the disputed 2000 elections exposed the many problems facing our election administration system, the League leaped into action. Bringing our coalition allies together, the League worked to ensure that key reforms were part of the congressional debate. In October 2002, the Help America Vote Act (HAVA) was signed into law, authorizing funds for each state to improve the operation of elections according to federal requirements.

The League continues to fight to ensure that the requirements of HAVA are implemented in ways to assure voter access. In 2005, the League created a public awareness campaign 5 Things You Need to Know on Election Day, designed to educate voters about the new requirements and the steps each voter could take to protect access. The campaign was highly successful, and has continued in subsequent election seasons with a particular emphasis on providing quality voting information to first-time voters and traditionally underrepresented communities.

Convention 2006 revised the League's stand on voting systems to assure that they would be secure, accurate, recountable, accessible and transparent.

Voter Protection in the 2000s - In 2006, the League launched its highly successful Public Advocacy for Voter Protection (PAVP) project and by the early 2010s, the PAVP project had expanded to more than 20 states as the League engaged in targeted state-based advocacy. The LWVUS collaborates with state Leagues to enhance their public education and advocacy campaigns to fight barriers to voter participation and to ensure election laws and processes are applied in a uniform and non-discriminatory manner.

Since its inception, the PAVP project has helped to remove or mitigate barriers to voting by underserved populations, and to advance the capacity of state Leagues to become even more effective advocates in five focus areas identified by the League as essential to protecting the votes of all citizens and improving election administration overall:

- Oppose photo ID and documentary proof of citizenship
- Improve administration of statewide database systems
- Guard against undue restrictions on voter registration
- Improve polling place management
- Improve poll worker training.

League work includes advocating for compliance with existing laws and regulations, such as the National Voter Registration Act of 1993, and advocating for key reforms through education and advocacy, and litigation when necessary. League action has been directed toward legislators, state/local elections officials, other policy makers, the media and concerned citizens, as appropriate.

One of the most major threats tackled by Leagues through the PAVP project is onerous and restrictive voter photo ID requirements. As many as 21 million Americans do not have government issued photo identification, with minorities and low-income individuals disproportionately less likely to have photo ID showing a current address. The League's efforts to combat voter suppression require issue monitoring and action by League advocates, often over multiple state legislative sessions, countless articles and opinion pieces placed in national and regional media, and multiple steps in the state and federal courts. League leaders and their partners have worked every step of the way to ensure that all eligible voters would have the opportunity to participate and have the tools necessary to overcome the confusion that results from these drawn-out battles.

During 2011-2012, the League's efforts resulted in the defeat of five strict voter photo ID bills during state legislative sessions (CO, IA, ME, MO and NC), in successful court action to block restrictive ID laws from implementation in four more states (SC, TX, PA and WI) and in the success of the People's Veto in ME in protecting same-day voter registration.

On Election Day 2012, Minnesota voters were the first in the country to soundly reject a proposed constitutional amendment that would have required government-issue voter photo ID and eliminated Election Day Registration in future elections. The League and its partners were instrumental in securing this success for voters.

In the late summer and fall of 2012, the League was also a leader in pushing back against illegal purging of voters from voter registration lists in Colorado and Florida. Finally, through additional court action, the League succeeded in overturning onerous restrictions on limits to independent voter registration in the state of Florida and quickly moved to fill the gap created by those restrictions.

The years 2013-2014 brought renewed attempts to restrict voting both nationally and in state legislatures. LWV staff assisted 31 state League affiliates as they encountered voter suppression issues. Leagues were instrumental in advocating against approximately 25 strict voter photo ID bills during the 2013-2014 state legislative sessions.

LWVUS and state Leagues across the country undertook court action to block restrictive laws in Kansas, North Carolina, Ohio, South Carolina, Wisconsin and many other states, with several major victories prior to Election Day 2016. Multiple legal challenges are still ongoing. An updated "ID Toolkit" was distributed to ensure that a unified, comprehensive and sustained message was disseminated by Leagues across the country. The toolkit includes: national overview of photo ID laws, overview of major court cases across the country, and a host of useful advocacy suggestions and templates.

The Ohio League received support in a challenge to reinstate the "golden week" of early voting following the legislature's action to cut it. In Georgia, a League-led coalition successfully stopped legislation that would have significantly reduced the early voting period.

In early 2013, the U.S. Supreme Court heard two important cases challenging the Voting Rights Act (VRA) and the National Voter Registration Act (NVRA), jeopardizing key voting rights safeguards that have been in place for decades. The LWVUS submitted an *amicus* brief in each case, and the Arizona state League was a plaintiff in the NVRA challenge. The League strongly supported the enforcement mechanism in the VRA, and, in support of the NVRA, continued its opposition to a documentary proof-of-citizenship requirement for voter registration.

During the 2014-2016 biennium, the LWVUS with state Leagues successfully challenged purging rules in Florida and sought to reverse a decision by the new Executive Director of the U.S. Election Assistance Commission to allow documentary proof-of-citizenship requirements in Kansas, Georgia and Arizona, which, if allowed, could set a precedent for other states to impose these restrictions.

State Leagues in Kansas, North Carolina, Ohio and Wisconsin were active participants and leaders in a variety of lawsuits seeking to block voting restrictions in those states.

Preventing Election Day Barriers

In the lead-up to Election Day 2016, League volunteers worked around the clock to protect the rights of voters. They staffed English and Spanish language hotlines answering voters' questions and troubleshooting for them. They set up poll observing programs, worked as poll workers and reported challenges to the national Election Protection Coalition. All of this was carried out with the goal of ensuring votes were successfully cast and counted. In states where restrictive photo ID laws had passed and were implemented, the League actively sought out individuals who could have difficulty getting the required ID for voting purposes to provide assistance. Assistance included education about the requirements, transportation to DMVs, and help in obtaining, and in some instances paying for underlying documentation (e.g. birth certificates). As part of this effort LWV printed tens of thousands of state-specific voter education materials in the lead-up to Election Day 2014. In 2016 alone, the League's work to protect and mobilize voters was featured in more than 35,000 news stories.

Leagues also regularly met with elections officials to encourage Election Day preparedness, poll worker training (especially in states where changes had been made), and fair distribution of resources so that all polling places are staffed and prepared for voters. Across the country hundreds of League volunteers staffed hotlines and worked as election observers to ensure voters' rights were protected on Election Day itself.

When possible, Leagues also worked to improve voter registration database matching criteria, students' right to vote using their campus address, increasing the effectiveness of public assistance office voter registration, and fair and equitable implementation of early voting and vote centers. Since 2013, LWVUS has promoted five key proactive election reform priorities:

- Secure online voter registration
- Permanent and portable statewide voter registration
- Expansion of early voting
- Improvement of polling place management
- Electronic streamlining of election processes.

Key Structures of Democracy

At the 2014 Convention, delegates voted an ambitious program to examine "Three Key Structures of Democracy": redistricting reform, amending the Constitution, and money in politics. Through League studies, new positions were developed on Money in Politics, Considerations for Evaluating Constitutional Amendment Proposals, and Constitutional Conventions under Article V of the U.S. Constitution. A League task force recommended a new position on

Redistricting to Convention 2016, and it was adopted by concurrence.

Based on these new positions and the positions on Voting Rights, the LWV launched a Campaign for Making Democracy Work for the 2016-2018 biennium. Voter registration, education, mobilization and protection are key parts of this campaign, which extends to legislative reform at the state and local levels as well as the national level.

VOTING RIGHTS

Citizen's Right to Vote

The right of every citizen to vote has been a basic League principle since its origin. Early on, many state Leagues adopted positions on election laws. But at the national level, despite a long history of protecting voting rights, the League found itself in the midst of the civil rights struggle of the 1960s without authority to take national legislative action on behalf of the Voting Rights Act of 1965.

Stung by the League's powerlessness to take action on such a significant issue, the 1970 Convention adopted a bylaws amendment enabling the League to act "to protect the right to vote of every citizen" without the formality of adopting voting rights in the national program. This unusual decision reflected member conviction that protecting the right to vote is indivisibly part of the League's basic purpose. When the 1974 Convention amended the Bylaws to provide that all League Principles could serve as authority for action, the separate amendment on voting rights was no longer needed.

The 1976 Convention's adoption of Voting Rights as an integral part of the national Program and the 1978 confirmation of that decision underlined the already existing authority under the Principles for the League to act on this basic right. In May 1982, the LWVUS Board made explicit the League's position on Voting Rights, and the 1982 Convention added Voting Rights to the national Program. The 1986 Convention affirmed that a key element of protecting the right to vote is encouraging participation in the political process. The 1990 Convention affirmed that the LWVUS should continue emphasis on protecting the right to vote by working to increase voter participation.

Leagues lobbied extensively for the 1970 amendments to the Voting Rights Act of 1965. In 1975, the League was part of a successful coalition effort to extend the act and expand its coverage to language minorities. In 1982, the League was a leader in the fight to strengthen the act and extend its major provisions for 25 years. In 1992, the League successfully sought reauthorization of the language assistance provision for an additional 15 years. In 2006, the League sponsored a major public initiative to support the Fannie Lou Hamer, Rosa Parks, and Coretta Scott King Voting Rights Act Reauthorization and Amendments Act of 2006. After months of action by Leagues across the country, the bill was passed and signed into law.

In response to threats to voting rights, the League has actively pursued litigation and administrative advocacy. In 1985, the League filed comments objecting to proposed regulations that would weaken the administrative enforcement provisions of Section 5 of the Act. And with other *amici curiae*, the League successfully urged the U.S. Supreme Court to adopt a strong interpretation of Section 2 for challenges to minority vote dilution.

From 1984 to 1989, building on a 1982 pilot project to monitor compliance with the Voting Rights Act in states covered by Section 5 of the Act, the League of Women Voters Education Fund (LWVEF) conducted projects to apply monitoring techniques in jurisdictions considering bailout from Section 5, to establish the League as a major source of information on bailout and compliance issues. Since 1988, the LWVEF worked with state and local Leagues to encourage full participation in the census and to ensure that subsequent reapportionment and redistrictings complied with one-person, one-vote requirements and the Voting Rights Act.

In 1996 and 1998, the LWVUS worked against congressional "English-only" legislation that would have effectively repealed the minority language provisions of the Voting Rights Act.

Increased accessibility to the electoral process is integral to ensuring a representative electoral process and the right of every citizen to vote. The League's grassroots campaign to secure national legislation to reform voter registration resulted in the 1990 House passage of the National Voter Registration Act (NVRA), "motor-voter," but the bill did not reach the Senate.

In 1991, the effort to pass national "motor-voter" legislation intensified, and the National Voter Registration Act of 1991 was introduced in the Senate. Leading a national coalition, the League executed a high visibility, multifaceted, grassroots drive, resulting in passage by both houses in 1992. But, the President vetoed the bill and the Senate failed to override.

In May 1993, the years of concerted effort by the League and other organizations paid off when both houses passed and the President signed the National Voter Registration Act. The President gave one of the signing pens to the LWVUS and saluted the League and other supporters as "fighters for freedom" in the continuing effort to expand American democracy. The "motor-voter" bill enabled citizens to apply to register at motor vehicle agencies automatically, as well as by mail and at public and private agencies that service the public.

League members quickly turned to ensuring effective implementation of the NVRA by states and key federal agencies. In early 1994, the LWVEF sponsored a "Motor Voter Alert" conference of representatives from more than 30 state Leagues, other grassroots activists, and representatives of civil rights and disability groups. Throughout 1994, while the LWVUS successfully lobbied the President and the Justice Department for strong federal leadership, state Leagues kept the pressure on their legislatures to pass effective enabling legislation by the January 1995 deadline. On September 12, 1994, the President issued an Executive Order requiring affected federal agencies to cooperate to the greatest extent possible with the states in implementing the law by providing funds, guidance and technical assistance to affected state public assistance agencies and agencies serving the disabled.

In 1995 and 1996, state and local Leagues worked to ensure effective state enforcement of the NVRA, as the LWVUS lobbied against congressional amendments that would have weakened or undermined the new federal law.

A report on the first-year impact of the NVRA indicated that 11 million citizens registered to vote under required NVRA motor voter, agency-based and mail-in programs in 1995. State Leagues and other organizations joined the Justice Department in filing lawsuits against states that refused to implement the NVRA. By summer 1996, Illinois, Pennsylvania, California, South Carolina, Virginia, Michigan and Kansas had lost Tenth Amendment states-rights arguments against the NVRA in federal court.

A noncompliance suit filed by the state League against New Hampshire was dropped early in 1996 when Congress passed a legislative rider exempting New Hampshire and Idaho from the NVRA by extending the law's deadline for state exemptions based on having election-day registration programs. The LWVUS opposed the New Hampshire exemption.

The LWVUS urged state elections officials and Congress to give the NVRA a chance to work before proposing changes. The League opposed a Senate NVRA "unfunded mandate" amendment that would have blocked state compliance by requiring the federal government to pay for implementation. The League also opposed amendments that required proof of citizenship to register to vote. All but the New Hampshire exemption were defeated or withdrawn.

As a complement, not a substitute, for the NVRA, the League continues to support shortening the period between registration and voting or same-day voter registration. The LWVUS has worked with state Leagues interested in promoting such reforms.

Despite the fact that the NVRA helped more Americans register to vote for the 1996 election than at any time since records have been kept, the LWVUS continued to fight congressional attempts to cripple the law. For example, the League lobbied and testified against the Voter Eligibility Verification Act, which sought to create a federal program to verify the citizenship of voter registrants and applicants,

arguing that the program was not necessary, would not work and would depress voter participation.

On related issues, the League has supported efforts to increase the accessibility of registration and voting for people with disabilities in federal elections and undertaken major efforts to encourage citizens to participate in the electoral process. Since 1988, the LWVEF has been coordinating broad-based voter registration drives for general elections, combining national publicity and outreach with grassroots activities by state and local Leagues, other groups and public officials. Since 2012, the League has served on the national working committee that oversees National Voter Registration Day, a major national initiative that has brought together thousands of partners to register hundreds of thousands of voters each September. In 2016, more than 350 Leagues from 45 states participated in National Voter Registration Day and registered more than 19,000 individuals to vote, making the League the single largest on-the-ground participant for the fifth year in a row.

The League also has worked to change aspects of the coverage and conduct of campaigns that may frustrate voter participation. From 1980-85, the LWVUS sought to pressure broadcasters not to air projections of election results before all the polls in a race have closed. In 1990, the LWVEF convened a symposium of scholars, journalists, campaign consultants and activists to examine the role of negative campaigning in the decline in voter participation and possible grassroots remedies.

The symposium led to a comprehensive effort to return the voter to the center of the election process. A campaign to "Take Back the System" coordinated League activities to make voter registration more accessible, provide voters with information about candidates and issues and restore voters' confidence and involvement in the electoral system. The program included LWVUS efforts on voter registration and campaign finance reform, an LWVEF presidential primary debate, a National Voter Registration Drive, voter registration efforts aimed at young citizens, a Campaign Watch pilot project to help citizens deter unfair campaign practices and grassroots efforts to register, inform and involve voters.

In 1994, the LWVEF launched a "Wired for Democracy" project, anticipating the potential of the Internet for providing voter education and opening government to citizens. In 1996, the League focused its energies to getting voters to the polls.

Original research sponsored by the LWVEF found that voters and nonvoters differ in several key respects: nonvoters are less likely to grasp the impact of elections on issues that matter to them, nonvoters are more likely to believe they lack information on which to base their voting decisions, nonvoters are more likely to perceive the voting process as difficult and cumbersome, and nonvoters are less likely to be contacted by organizations encouraging them to vote.

In 1996, Leagues nationwide conducted targeted, grassroots get-out-the-vote (GOTV) campaigns armed with this message, "It's about your children's education, your taxes, your Social Security, your Medicare and your safe streets. It's about you and your family. Vote." Focusing on racial and ethnic minorities and other underrepresented populations, Leagues worked in coalition with other organizations to expand their reach and let voters know they have a stake in the system. Despite an overall downturn in voter participation in 1996, precincts targeted by the League's effort posted increased voting rates.

In the 2000 elections, the LWVEF worked with state and local Leagues on intensive GOTV campaigns in 30 communities, targeting underrepresented voters. Training highlighted new ways to engage citizens to work in coalitions with diverse communities. The League also participated in forming Youth Vote 2000, a nonpartisan coalition of organizations committed to encouraging greater participation in the political process and promoting a better understanding of public policy issues among youth.

Also in 2000, the League launched its "Take a Friend to Vote" (TAFTV) campaign, based on research showing that nonvoters are most likely to vote if asked by a friend, family member, neighbor or someone else whom they respect. The TAFTV campaign featured toolkits with reminder postcards and bumper stickers, a website, PSAs on Lifetime Television and "advertorials" in major magazines featuring celebrities and their friends talking about the importance of voting.

In 1998, the League tested two online systems to make trustworthy, nonpartisan election information readily available to web users. The LWVEF chose the DemocracyNet (DNet) as its nationwide online voter information platform and worked with state and local Leagues to expand the system to all 50 states for the 2000 elections. By the 2004 election, DNet was the most comprehensive source of voter information and one of the top online sites for unbiased election information, offering full coverage of all federal elections as well as thousands of state and local candidates. VOTE411 replaced DNet in 2006. In 2016, nearly 4.5 million users visited VOTE411 to find the most up to date facts to help them overcome confusion and have the information they need to cast a vote.

When the 2000 election exposed the many problems facing the election system, the League began to work relentlessly on election reform and bringing its importance to national attention. The LWVUS helped draft and pass the Help America Vote Act of 2002 (HAVA), working closely with a civil rights coalition in developing amendments and lobbying for key provisions.

The LWVUS took a leadership role in forming an election reform coalition to develop recommendations on HAVA implementation and testified before both houses, stressing the importance of substantial new federal funding for election reform efforts. The League used its special expertise to argue for improved voting systems and machines, provisional balloting and other safeguards, and improvements in voter registration systems and poll worker training and administration.

The LWVEF worked to heighten public awareness about election administration problems and to provide informational and action materials to state and local Leagues. In 2001, the LWVEF hosted three "Focus on the Voter" symposia and worked with Leagues to design and complete a survey of election administration practices in local jurisdictions. Four hundred and sixty Leagues from 47 states and the District of Columbia responded to the survey. A report of the findings was released at a post-election symposium in November 2001, and it concluded that "good enough is not good enough."

In 2001 and 2002, *Election Administration Reform: A Leader's Guide for Action,* the *Election 2001 Toolkit* and *Navigating Election Day: What Every Voter Needs to Know* were made available to state and local Leagues for voter education activities. In late 2002, the LWVEF convened a conference, sponsored by the McCormick Tribune Foundation, to explore emerging issues in election reform.

In the 108th Congress, the key issue was funding for HAVA, as the President initially proposed that HAVA not be fully funded. A joint lobbying effort of state and local government organizations, civil rights groups and the League prevailed in achieving full funding for the first two years of implementation.

In mid-2003, the LWVUS published *Helping America Vote: Implementing the New Federal Provisional Ballot Requirement,* which examined and made key policy recommendations for states and localities in implementing HAVA's provisional balloting requirement. Another report followed in 2004, *Helping America Vote: Safeguarding the Vote,* which outlined a set of recommended operational and management practices for state and local elections officials to enhance voting system security, protect eligible voters, and ensure that valid votes are counted.

Also in 2004, the League of Women Voters conducted a survey of local and state elections officials in a number of targeted states to identify potential problems with HAVA implementation that could put the votes of eligible voters at risk. The League identified the *Top Five Risks to Eligible Voters in 2004,* including voter registration problems, erroneous purging, problems with the new voter ID requirement, difficulties with voting systems and a failure to count provisional ballots, and asked elections officials for resolution before the election. League leaders in various states were at the forefront of high-profile battles over HAVA's implementation.

In 2006, the League released *Thinking Outside the Ballot Box: Innovations at the Polling Place,* a comprehensive report aimed at sharing successful election administration stories with local officials throughout the country.

The League's respected voter education tool, *Choosing the President: A Citizen's Guide to the Electoral Process,* was revised in 2004 and 2008. The 2008 edition was also translated into Russian and Arabic and was the basis for *Electing the President,* a 16-page education supplement created and distributed to schools in collaboration with the Newspapers in Education Institute. *Electing the President* was updated in 2012 and again in 2016 and distributed to schools in collaboration with the Newspapers in Education Institute.

In every major election year since 2004 the League has made available its attractive *VOTE* brochure, a succinct, step-by-step guide to voting and Election Day, designed to reach out to new, young and first time voters. The *5 Things You Need to Know on Election Day* card has also provided hundreds of thousands of voters with simple steps to ensure their vote is counted. The brochure and card continue to be popular and useful to the present.

At the 2004 Convention, the League determined that in order to ensure integrity and voter confidence in elections, the LWVUS supports the implementation of voting systems and procedures that are secure, accurate, recountable and accessible. State and local Leagues may support a particular voting system appropriate to their area, but should evaluate them based on the "secure, accurate, recountable and accessible" criteria. Leagues should consult with the LWVUS before taking a stand on a specific type of voting system to ensure that the League speaks consistently.

At Convention 2006, delegates further clarified this position with a resolution stating that the Citizens' Right to Vote be interpreted to affirm that the LWVUS supports only voting systems that are designed so that:

- They employ a voter-verifiable paper ballot or other paper record, said paper being the official record of the voter's intent.
- The voter can verify, either by eye or with the aid of suitable devices for those who have impaired vision, that the paper ballot/record accurately reflects his or her intent.

- Such verification takes place while the voter is still in the process of voting.
- The paper ballot/record is used for audits and recounts.
- The vote totals can be verified by an independent hand count of the paper ballot/record.
- Routine audits of the paper ballot/record in randomly selected precincts can be conducted in every election, and the results published by the jurisdiction.

At Convention 2010, delegates added the principle of transparency, so that the League would support voting systems that are secure, accurate, recountable, accessible and transparent.

In 2006, the League launched VOTE411.org, a "one-stop-shop" for election related information, providing nonpartisan information to the public with both general and state-specific information including a nationwide polling place locator, absentee ballot information, ballot measure information, etc. In 2008 and 2012, the LWVUS accomplished consecutive overhauls and improvements to this award-winning voter education website, making it the most comprehensive, easy-to-use online tool for voters. The site is at the heart of the League's campaign to prepare voters.

Since launching VOTE411 in 2006, approximately 34 million people have benefited from the information available on the site. This support has seen expanded access to information about candidates at the state and local levels with every consecutive election year. In partnership with hundreds of state and local Leagues, VOTE411 has successfully provided voters with information on where tens of thousands of candidates stand on the issues and up-to-date election rules for all 50 states in every election year. One hundred percent of voters who visited VOTE411 before the 2016 general election were able to find a partial listing of the candidates that would be on their ballot and approximately 70% of voters found a complete ballot. And for the first time in 2016, the statements from the Presidential candidates were available in English and Spanish languages.

The League president testifies regularly before the U.S. Election Assistance Commission and congressional committees, providing feedback on the success of HAVA implementation and other voting issues nationwide.

In 2006, the League also launched the Public Advocacy for Voter Protection (PAVP) project, and the League has undertaken concerted nationwide efforts to promote voter protection and education to prevent the development of processes and laws that threaten to disenfranchise voters, to educate the public on new election procedures, and provide voters with the information they need to cast a vote and be sure that vote is counted. The period 2014-2016 brought unprecedented challenges, and successes, to the PAVP program, with participating Leagues ultimately defeating dozens of onerous barriers that threatened the right to vote. In 2016 for the first time, LWVEF supported state League's efforts to call more than 100,000 people to encourage their participation in the 2016 election and make sure they had accurate information about early voting and identification rules.

As part of the PAVP effort, in 2007, the League opposed state legislation that would require documentary proof of citizenship or picture ID to register to vote, as well as to vote. The League also filed a "friend-of-the-court" brief in a Supreme Court case regarding ID requirements in Indiana. In 2009, the League filed an *amicus* brief in the Arizona voter ID case, *Gonzalez v. Arizona,* asking the 9th Circuit Court of Appeals to recognize that the National Voter Registration Act of 1993 prohibits a proof-of-citizenship requirement when using the national mail voter registration application form. The League again filed an *amicus* brief when the case was finally argued before the Supreme Court in 2013. The League and its allies finally prevailed. In the renamed *ITCA v. Arizona,* the Court agreed that the NVRA preempts state law. For more PAVP project information see page 9 above.

In 2008, the League worked to support voting rights by publicly requesting that Secretaries of State across the country designate veterans' health facilities as voter registration agencies as provided for in the National Voter Registration Act. In 2012-2014 this work continued as LWVUS and many state Leagues worked to ensure the state healthcare exchanges created under the Affordable Care Act were designated as voter registration agencies.

In 2008, the LWVEF produced *Engaging New Citizens as New Voters: A Guide to Naturalization Ceremonies,* which detailed how Leagues could get involved in such ceremonies. In 2012, LWVEF built off this effort and supported targeted local Leagues with grant funding and strategic support in order to successfully register new citizens at naturalization ceremonies and underrepresented community colleges. In 2014, LWVEF released a brand-new toolkit designed to support Leagues in their work to engage new citizens as first-time voters. Leveraging this new toolkit in 2016, LWVEF launched its largest nationwide grant funded effort to support state and local Leagues in registering newly naturalized citizens, ultimately resulting in in tens of thousands of new registrants at hundreds of citizenship ceremonies nationwide.

In 2008, an Election Audit Task Force was appointed to report to the LWVUS Board on the auditing of election procedures and processes. The 2009 report is available at www.lwv.org. Leagues should find this report useful in talking with their legislatures and elections officials about election auditing.

Since 2010, the League has aimed through its national Youth Voter Registration project to bring more young people, especially in communities of color, into the democratic process. Local Leagues in dozens of targeted communities have received LWVEF grant funding and strategic support to successfully assist tens of thousands of students to register to vote. The League used data and feedback provided by participating Leagues to determine effective strategies and produced a groundbreaking and widely utilized 2011 training manual "Empowering the Voters of Tomorrow" for Leagues and other groups interested in registering high school students. The guide was updated and republished in early 2013 and again in 2015.

All aspects of the League's 2012-2016 work was encompassed into one major national initiative entitled Power the Vote. Through the Power the Vote effort, Leagues worked at all levels to leverage resources and the League's powerful voice to protect, register, educate and mobilize voters to participate. The League's 2012-2014 efforts are summarized in the whitepaper *Power the Vote: How a new initiative launched results for millions of voters.* It and many corresponding training and planning resources are available at www.lwv.org.

In 2013, the Supreme Court in the case of *Shelby County v. Holder* reversed key voting rights protections that had been in place for decades. The Court ruled that the Voting Rights Act (VRA) formula for determining which jurisdictions would have to clear their election law changes with the federal government was based on old data and was therefore unconstitutional.

The League immediately took action urging Congress to repair and restore the effectiveness of the VRA. This work continued into 2015 and 2016, with active participation from state and local Leagues in targeted districts backing up the LWVUS lobbying efforts to enact a new Voting Rights Advancement Act, restoring key elements of the VRA while extending new protections nationwide.

Also in the 2010s, Leagues worked in their state legislatures with other concerned organizations for bills to re-enfranchise former felons, believing that excessive disenfranchisement undermines voting rights as well as the reintegration of former felon into the community.

THE LEAGUE'S POSITION

The League of Women Voters believes voting is a fundamental citizen right that must be guaranteed.

Statement of Position on Citizen's Right to Vote, as Announced by National Board, March 1982.

DC Self-Government and Full Voting Representation

The League of Women Voters, born in 1920 out of the struggle to get the vote for women, began early to seek redress for another disenfranchised group: the citizens of the District of Columbia (DC). The League has supported DC self-government since 1938. Realization of these goals has been slow, but, since 1961, DC residents have made some gains in the drive for full citizenship rights. The remaining goals of voting representation in both the House and Senate and full home-rule powers were made explicit in the LWVUS program in March 1982.

The League has applied a wide variety of techniques, including a massive petition campaign in 1970, to persuade Congress to change the status of the "Last Colony." League support has been behind each hard-won step: in 1961, the right of DC citizens to vote for President and Vice-President through ratification of the 23rd Amendment to the Constitution; in 1970, the right to elect a nonvoting delegate to Congress; and in 1974, a limited home-rule charter providing for an elected mayor and city council, based on the 1973 District of Columbia Self Government and Governmental Reorganization Act. The League supported the last two reforms as interim steps until voting representation in Congress and full home-rule powers are achieved.

On August 22, 1978, the Senate confirmed the House-approved constitutional amendment providing full voting representation in Congress for DC citizens. State and local Leagues took the lead in ratification efforts. However, when the ratification period expired in 1985, only 16 states of the necessary 38 had ratified the amendment.

In 1993, at the request of the LWV of the District of Columbia, the LWVUS Board agreed that DC statehood would "afford the same rights of self-government and full voting representation" for DC citizens as for other U.S. citizens. Accordingly, the League endorsed statehood as one way of implementing the national League position.

The LWVUS was instrumental in the formation of the Coalition for DC Representation in Congress (now DC Vote), which seeks to build a national political movement supporting full representation in Congress and full home-rule powers for the citizens of DC.

Convention 2000 adopted a concurrence to add to the LWVUS position support for the "restoration of an annual, predictable federal payment to the District to compensate for revenues denied and expenses incurred because of the federal presence."

In April 2000, the LWVUS Board agreed that the existing LWVUS position on DC voting rights also includes support for autonomy for the District in budgeting locally raised revenue and for eliminating the annual congressional DC appropriations budget-approval process. While such congressional review remains in force, the League continues to urge members of Congress to oppose appropriations bills that undermine the right of self-government of DC citizens, including restrictions on abortion funding.

In the 108th Congress, the League worked with DC Vote to develop legislation providing voting rights in Congress to DC residents. A hearing was held in spring 2004 to discuss four different legislative approaches to gaining representation in Congress.

In 2005, members of Congress took the DC voting rights issue on with more enthusiasm than had been seen in years. Under a new legislative plan, Utah would receive an additional fourth seat in Congress while congressional voting rights in the House of Representatives would be provided for American citizens living in Washington, DC. This balanced approach, developed by Rep. Tom Davis (R-VA) and supported by the DC City Council and Mayor, would provide voting rights for District citizens without upsetting the partisan balance of the House.

As momentum for this plan increased, the League worked tirelessly to encourage members of Congress and the public to take action on DC voting rights.

In 2006, the League continued to work hard in support of the proposed plan. The League president traveled to Ohio to tell key Congressmen that their leadership was vital to the future of DC voting rights. While in Ohio, the president met with members, voters and the media to shed light on the DC voting rights issue.

At the same time, the LWVEF launched a DC Voting Rights Education project, aimed at building public awareness of the unique relationship between Congress and DC citizens, specifically the lack of full voting rights. As part of the project, selected Leagues throughout the country began work to educate voters and local leaders on the DC voting rights issue through summer 2007.

Despite the League's hard work and progress in the 109th and 110th Congress toward passing DC voting rights legislation to provide House voting rights to District voters, success ultimately eluded supporters.

The League of Women Voters believes that citizens of the District of Columbia should be afforded the same rights of self-government and full voting representation in Congress as are all other citizens of the United States. The LWVUS supports restoration of an annual, predictable federal payment to the District to compensate for revenues denied and expenses incurred because of the federal presence.

Statement of Position on DC Self-Government and Full Voting Representation, as Revised by National Board, March 1982 and June 2000.

THE ELECTION PROCESS

Apportionment

The apportionment of election districts was a state issue until 1962 and 1964 Supreme Court rulings, requiring that both houses of state legislatures must be apportioned substantially on population, transferred the issue to the national arena. These rulings, spelling out the basic constitutional right to equal representation, prompted introduction in Congress of constitutional amendments and laws to subvert the Court's one-person, one-vote doctrine. Leagues in 33 states already had positions on the issue when, in 1965, the League's national council adopted a study on apportionment. By January 1966, the League had reached national member agreement on a position that both houses of state legislatures must be apportioned substantially on population. The 1972 Convention extended the position to cover all voting districts.

League action on both the national and state levels during the late 1960s had a significant role in the defeat of efforts to circumvent the Court's ruling. The League first lobbied in Congress against the Dirksen Amendment, which would have allowed apportionment of one legislative house based on factors other than population, and later worked to defeat resolutions to amend the Constitution by petition of

state legislatures for a constitutional Convention. Successful efforts to fend off inadvisable constitutional amendments have left the responsibility for work on this position at the state and local levels. Successive League Conventions have reaffirmed the commitment to an LWVUS Apportionment position to be available for action should the need arise. After the 1980 census, state and local Leagues used this position to work for equitable apportionment of state and local representative bodies.

Leagues conducted projects to encourage the widest possible participation in the 1990 census as a way to ensure the most accurate population base for apportionment and redistricting. Leagues also work for equitable apportionment and redistricting of all elected government bodies, using techniques from public education and testimony to monitoring and litigation.

Behind the League position on Apportionment is a conviction that a population standard is the most equitable way of assuring that each vote is of equal value in a democratic and representative system of government. The term "substantially" used in Supreme Court decisions allows adequate leeway for districting to provide for any necessary local diversities, and to protect minority representation under the League's Voting Rights position.

In 1998-99, the League urged Congress to fully fund the 2000 census and to support scientific sampling as the means to ensure the most accurate count. State Leagues also have worked to ensure that scientific sampling is used for redistricting within the states.

In 2009, the LWVEF was an official partner of the U.S. Census, with the goal of getting everyone counted. LWVEF staff worked closely with national partners (such as civil rights and Latino groups), and provided information and support to state and local Leagues in their efforts to minimize an undercount.

THE LEAGUE'S POSITION
The League of Women Voters believes that congressional districts and government legislative bodies should be apportioned substantially on population.

The League is convinced that this standard, established by the Supreme Court, should be maintained and that the U.S. Constitution should not be amended to allow for consideration of factors other than population in apportionment.

Statement of Position on Apportionment, as Announced by National Board, January 1966 and Revised March 1982.

See also the position on Voting Rights, which applies to apportionment issues. Leagues applying the Apportionment Position should be aware that the Voting Rights position (and League action supporting the Voting Rights Act) recognizes that both the Constitution and the Voting Rights Act require that reapportionment not dilute the effective representation of minority citizens.

Redistricting

Political and racial gerrymandering distorts and undermines representative democracy by allowing officials to select their voters rather than voters to elect their officials. When done for purposes of racial discrimination or to ensure the dominance of one political party, or even to ensure the election of a particular legislator, gerrymandering runs counter to equal voting rights for all.

For much of the League's history, redistricting has been seen as a state and local issue, but as state Leagues have become more active and the political gerrymandering of the U.S. Congress has become more apparent, the LWVUS has provided assistance and, in the 2014-2016 biennium, developed a nationwide position statement.

In 2005, the national Board affirmed that Leagues at all levels may take action under LWVUS positions relating to redistricting. Using the positions on "Apportionment," "Citizen's Right to Vote," and "Congress," Leagues should work to achieve three goals consistent with those positions:

- Congressional districts and government legislative bodies should be apportioned substantially on population ("one person, one vote").

- Redistricting should not dilute the effective representation of minority citizens.
- Efforts that attempt or result in partisan gerrymandering should be opposed.

In 2006, the League joined other groups in holding a nonpartisan redistricting conference in Salt Lake City, Utah. As a result of that meeting, the League and partners released a report "Building a National Redistricting Reform Movement" which looks at lessons learned from unsuccessful redistricting reform attempts in 2005 and suggests strategies to pursue and pitfalls to avoid in future reform efforts.

Leagues across the country continue to press for redistricting reform at the state level and the LWVUS has gone to the Supreme Court with "friend-of-the-court" briefs in landmark cases against political and racial gerrymandering. In 2009, the LWVEF hosted a unique redistricting conference that brought together experts and stakeholders from across the nation to discuss how to work together to influence the results of the state redistricting processes following the 2010 Census. The participants agreed upon several core principles and wrote a report emphasizing the importance of transparency in the redistricting process.

In the 2010s, the League expressed concern about "prison-based gerrymandering" in which inmates are counted as residents in the district where the prison is located instead of at their home addresses. Working with other organizations, the League sought better information from the Census to support the push to end such gerrymandering.

In 2011 and 2012, state Leagues played pivotal roles in advocating for improved redistricting processes through a nationwide funded Shining a Light project. Leagues hosted public events, delivered much-quoted testimony before decision-making bodies, presented alternative maps, launched major public education and media campaigns, and engaged key allies to promote transparent and fair redistricting processes. Key League priorities included: advocating for adequate public comment periods before *and* after the introduction of redistricting proposals; disclosure of committee timelines and other important details; and opportunities for community groups, especially those representing diverse voices, to get involved.

Following the 2011 redistricting process, several state Leagues engaged in litigation or statewide ballot initiative campaigns to challenge unsatisfactory redistricting outcomes. The Texas League and LWVEF jointly submitted comments urging the US Department of Justice to object to VRA Section 5 preclearance of what the League deemed a discriminatory redistricting proposal. Elsewhere, the North Carolina League joined other civil rights groups in challenging a redistricting plan that would negatively impact minority and other voters, the Arizona League filed an *amicus* brief which successfully urged the state Supreme Court to protect that state's independent redistricting commission, and the Pennsylvania League participated in a successful citizen's appeal of a state plan.

In California, League leaders worked throughout 2011 and 2012 to defend and ensure success for that state's new Independent Citizens Commission process in California, and also provided a detailed analysis and recommendations for future redistricting commissions. In Florida, the League spearheaded multiple legislative and legal efforts to ensure that the integrity of new, groundbreaking redistricting criteria would be upheld. The League prevailed in court when it challenged the 2010 redistricting plan for violating the new criteria. The Florida League garnered an impressive array of statewide and national media coverage for its efforts.

In Ohio, the League led a high-profile yet ultimately unsuccessful effort to pass a November 2012 ballot initiative that would have instituted an independent redistricting commission.

Public opinion polling has shown high public support for taking the redistricting process out of the hands of partisan legislatures, and many Leagues continue to consider how best to achieve more representative processes. Leagues remain engaged in pending legal challenges or appeals in several states and continue to pursue a range of reform opportunities to reform the redistricting process. In early 2012, LWVEF published "Shining a Light: Redistricting Lessons Learned," which lays out key League priorities related to redistricting reform. The publication has been shared widely with Leagues and partners nationwide.

Wishing to give redistricting a higher profile for League action, the 2014 national program on Key Structures of Democracy called for a Task Force on Redistricting which surveyed existing state League positions and recommended a new concurrence statement to the 2016 convention.

THE LEAGUE'S POSITION

The League of Women Voters believes responsibility for redistricting preferably should be vested in an independent special commission, with membership that reflects the diversity of the unit of government, including citizens at large, representatives of public interest groups, and members of minority groups.

Every redistricting process should include:

- **Specific timelines for the steps leading to a redistricting plan**
- **Full disclosure throughout the process and public hearings on the plan proposed for adoption**
  - **Redistricting at all levels of government must be accomplished in an open, unbiased manner with citizen participation and access at all levels and steps of the process, and**
  - **Should be subject to open meeting laws.**
- **A provision that any redistricting plan should be adopted by the redistricting authority with more than a simple majority vote.**
  - **Remedial provisions established in the event that the redistricting authority fails to enact a plan. Specific provisions should be made for court review of redistricting measures and for courts to require the redistricting authority to act on a specific schedule.**
    - **Time limits should be set for initiating court action for review.**
    - **The courts should promptly review and rule on any challenge to a redistricting plan and require adjustments if the standards have not been met.**

The standards on which a redistricting plan is based, and on which any plan should be judged, must:

- Be enforceable in court
- Require:
  - Substantially equal population
  - Geographic contiguity
  - Effective representation of racial and linguistic minorities
- Provide for (to the extent possible)
  - Promotion of partisan fairness
  - Preservation and protection of "communities of interest"
  - Respect for boundaries of municipalities and counties
- Compactness and competitiveness may also be considered as criteria so long as they do not conflict with the above criteria
- Explicitly reject
  - Protection of incumbents, through such devices as considering an incumbent's address
  - Preferential treatment for a political party, through such devices as considering party affiliation, voting history and candidate residence.

Statement of Position on Redistricting, as Adopted by Concurrence, June 2016. This position does not supersede any existing state League redistricting position.

Money in Politics

After the 1972 Convention approved "further study of Congress," the 1973 Council—spurred by spending abuses in congressional and presidential campaigns—focused on campaign finance. Accelerated study and agreement in 1973 led to the Campaign Finance position, which applied League Principles supporting an open and representative government to political campaigns.

The League initiated a petition drive and lobbied intensively for the campaign reforms embodied in the Federal Election Campaign Act of 1974 (FECA). When the law was challenged in court, the League, together with other organizations, intervened as defendants. In 1976, the Supreme Court upheld portions of the law providing for disclosure, public financing and contribution limits, but it overturned limits on candidates' spending, if they used private financing, and limits on independent expenditures. The Court also ruled that the method of selection of the Federal Election Commission (FEC) was unconstitutional, because it allowed Congress to encroach on the President's appointment power. After the Court's decision, the League successfully lobbied for a new law creating an independent and constitutionally acceptable FEC.

In response to budget attacks on the FEC in the 104th Congress, the League testified and lobbied in support of the FEC's Fiscal Year 1997 budget request and against efforts to undermine the agency's core enforcement and disclosure programs through funding cuts.

The League's position on Campaign Finance reflects continuing concern for open and honest elections and for maximum citizen participation in the political process. The League's campaign finance reform strategy has two tracks:

- Achieve incremental reforms where possible in the short-term
- Build support for public financing as the best long-term solution.

Although provided under current law for presidential elections, public funding of congressional elections, which the League supports, has been an elusive goal. Current law does embody other League goals: full and timely disclosure of campaign contributions and expenditures; one central committee to coordinate, control and report financial transactions for each candidate, party or other committee; an independent body to monitor and enforce the law; and the encouragement of broad-based contributions from citizens.

The League continues to look for ways to limit the size and type of contributions from all sources as a means of combating undue influence in the election process. League action on this issue is built on a careful assessment of all proposed changes in campaign financing law. The League continues to assess proposals to equalize government services for challengers and incumbents so that candidates can compete more equitably. The League favors shortening the time period between primaries and general elections.

In 1989-1992, the League fought for comprehensive campaign finance reform to address the abuses in the existing system, supporting bills that curbed special-interest contributions and provided public financing for candidates who accepted voluntary spending limits. The League called for limits to donations from political action committees (PAC) and large contributors, for closing the soft-money loophole and for public benefits for candidates such as reduced postage and reduced broadcasting costs.

Both houses of Congress enacted reform bills in 1990, but a conference committee was unable to resolve the differences before adjournment of the 101st Congress. Both houses passed strong reform measures in 1992, and the bill that emerged from the conference committee promised the most far-reaching campaign finance reform since Watergate. The President vetoed the bill, and an attempt to override was unsuccessful.

In 1991-1992, the League defended the system of public financing for presidential candidates through check-offs on income tax forms. Faced with an impending shortfall in the Presidential Election Campaign Fund, the League countered with an attack on many fronts: an appeal to taxpayers and preparers to use the check-off; testimony before the House Elections Subcommittee to increase the check-off from $1.00 to $3.00, with indexing for inflation; opposition to IRS regulations that would weaken the system; support for a House bill guaranteeing matching funds for qualified presidential primary candidates; and participation in an *amicus curiae* challenging, unsuccessfully, Treasury Department regulations that subvert the language and congressional intent of the presidential public financing system.

In 1993, the presidential check-off was increased to $3.00, with support from the League, assuring continued viability for the fund. The League also supported comprehensive campaign finance reform, which stalled in partisan wrangling.

In 1995 and 1996, the League continued its support for comprehensive reform through lobbying, testimony, grassroots action and work with the media. Members pushed for voluntary spending limits; public benefits, such as reduced-cost broadcasting and postal services, for participating candidates; aggregate limits on the total amounts candidates could receive from political action committees (PACs) and large individual contributions; and closing the loopholes that allow huge amounts of special-interest money to influence the system.

Also in this period, the LWVEF launched a comprehensive program for articulating a public voice on campaign finance. The Money + Politics: People Change the Equation project brought citizens together to debate the problems in the system and discuss possible solutions.

In 1996, opponents of League-favored reforms, arguing that politics is underfunded, sought to increase the amounts of special-interest money flowing into the system by loosening many existing contribution limits. The League and its allies soundly defeated this approach in the House but were unable to overcome opposition from most congressional leaders in both parties. Reformers did build bipartisan support for reform outside the leadership circles.

The near collapse of the federal campaign finance system during the 1996 election focused national attention on the need for reform. In December 1996, the LWVUS endorsed the goals of a reform proposal developed by a group of academics. The approach focused on closing gaping loopholes in the law that allow special interests, the political parties and others to channel hundreds of millions of dollars into candidates' campaigns. Among the key goals: a ban on "soft money," closing the sham issue advocacy loophole and improving disclosure and enforcement.

The LWVEF mounted a major advertising and grassroots education initiative calling attention to achievable campaign reforms. Working with experts from diverse political views, the LWVEF published a blueprint for reform: *5 Ideas for Practical Campaign Reform*. Other efforts included ads in major newspapers, a PSA featuring national news anchor Walter Cronkite and citizen caucuses in 20 states.

An unrelenting push by the LWVUS and other reform advocates succeeded in shifting the campaign-finance debate in the 105th Congress from a deadlock over spending limits to real movement to close the most egregious loopholes.

The League supported the bipartisan McCain-Feingold bill in the Senate and the counterpart Shays-Meehan bill in the House, bringing grassroots pressure to bear against efforts by congressional leaders to stonewall real reform. Leagues responded to Action Alerts and lobbied their members of Congress to defeat parliamentary maneuvers blocking votes and to support meaningful reform.

In summer 1998, reformers succeeded in forcing the House Speaker to schedule a vote on reform bills, including Shays-Meehan. Despite concerted efforts to defeat it, the bill passed the House by a vote of 252-179 in August 1998. League members immediately urged senators to support a cloture vote on campaign finance reform legislation and to vote for real reform. However, in September 1998 the Senate once again failed to break a filibuster preventing a vote.

In 1998, the LWVEF launched a campaign finance reform project Strategies for Success in the Midwest, working with state Leagues in Illinois, Indiana, Iowa, Michigan, Minnesota, Ohio and Wisconsin. Efforts focused on educating citizens on practical ways to reform campaign finance and to offer citizens an opportunity to participate in the debate. In 1999, the LWVEF distributed "Make the Link" materials to state Leagues, drawing the connection between campaign finance and key issues such as the environment, teen smoking and health care.

On the Hill, House leaders again worked to block the Shays-Meehan bill in the 106th Congress. Using a discharge petition, reformers forced the leadership to move, and the bill passed on a strong vote. Senate passage once again proved elusive, despite citizen pressure. However, the League and other supporters were successful in achieving passage in June 2000 of so-called "527" legislation, requiring political organizations set up under Section 527 of the IRS code to disclose the identity and amounts given by their donors and how they spend the money.

As the League continued to focus on reducing the corrupting influence of big money in elections, League work at the state level contributed to real progress. Public financing, the "Clean Money Option," was adopted in several states, including Arizona and Maine; other state reform efforts have made progress in Massachusetts and Vermont. Reform measures were on the 2000 ballot in Missouri and Oregon, but fell short.

The LWV and other reformers succeeded in putting campaign finance reform on the front burner of the national political agenda. In January 2000, in *Nixon v. Shrink Missouri PAC*, the Supreme Court upheld limits on state campaign contributions that were analogous to the federal limits. The LWVUS joined an *amicus* brief in the case. The Court's decision restated the constitutional underpinning for campaign finance reform formulated in *Buckley v. Valeo*, despite arguments by reform opponents.

In 1999-2000, League members supported 90-year-old Doris Haddock, "Granny D," in her walk across the country to promote campaign finance reform.

The battle for meaningful campaign finance reform has been long and hard. The Senate debated the McCain-Feingold-Shays-Meehan bill for more than a week in 2001. The League pushed successfully for the strengthening amendment from Senator Wellstone (D-MN) and to protect against a raft of weakening amendments. On the House side, the leadership once again tried to use the rules to block reform. Our allies in the House, with strong support from the LWVUS, had to resort to a discharge petition to force action.

The LWVUS worked with the bill's sponsors and lobbied swing members of the House and Senate to achieve campaign finance reform. The LWVUS conducted two rounds of phone banking, asking League members in key districts to lobby at key junctures in the congressional debate. The LWV participated in many press conferences and rallies to make the citizen's voice heard on campaign finance reform.

On March 27, 2002, the League's five-year campaign for the McCain-Feingold-Shays-Meehan bill reached fruition when the President signed the legislation into law. The bill, which became known as the Bipartisan Campaign Reform Act (BCRA), closed the most significant loopholes in campaign finance regulation: the "soft money" loophole that allowed unlimited corporate, union and individual contributions and the "sham issue ad" loophole that allowed undisclosed contributions to campaign advertising advocating particular candidates. The League was instrumental in developing this approach and pushing it at the grassroots and in Congress to final enactment.

With the passage of BCRA, the League turned its attention to legal challenges to the law, which continue to the present day. The LWVUS filed an *amicus* brief on "sham issue ads" for the Supreme Court case *McConnell v. FEC*. The brief explained why it is important that funding for attack ads in the final days of an election not be used to circumvent the "soft money" ban in BCRA. In September 2003, the League organized a rally at the Supreme Court to demonstrate public support for the law. In December, the Supreme Court upheld all the key components of BCRA in *McConnell v. FEC*, including the "sham issue ad" provisions briefed by League.

In the first half of the 108th Congress, the League urged Senators to cosponsor the "Our Democracy, Our Airwaves Act" introduced by Senators McCain, Feingold and Durbin. The LWVUS helped targeted Leagues organize in-district lobby visits in support of the Act, and through the National Lobby Corps lobbied selected Senators requesting co-sponsorship of the bill.

The League, along with partners, conducted a national public education campaign "Our Democracy, Our Airwaves," studying the role of television in elections, the cost of accessing these public airwaves and the importance of strengthening public interest information coming from broadcasters. The LWVUS put together organizing tools for local Leagues to use while creating educational campaigns in their communities.

In the second session of the 108th Congress, the League continued its work on improving the presidential public financing system. The LWVUS sought cosponsors to legislation introduced by Senators McCain and Feingold and Representatives Shays and Meehan to fix the system. The LWVUS also joined a coalition project that sought pledge commitments from the 2004 presidential candidates to support the public financing system's reform if elected. In 2003 and 2004, the League again urged taxpayers to check the box to support the Presidential Election Fund.

In 2005 and 2006, the League continued to promote campaign finance reform as well as public funding for presidential elections. In December 2005, the League president spoke at a Capitol Hill conference titled "The Issue of Presidential Public Financing: Its Goals, History, Current Status and Problems." In 2006, the LWVUS joined with other organizations in a letter to U.S. Representatives urging them to cosponsor and support the Meehan-Shays bill that would make a series of important reforms to the presidential public financing system.

Throughout 2005, the League urged members of Congress to vote against the Pence-Wynn and other bills that aimed to undermine existing campaign finance regulations. In December, the League joined other groups in submitting an *amicus* brief in the Supreme Court case *Wisconsin Right to Life, Inc. v. Federal Election Commission,* which challenged the application of the Bipartisan Campaign Reform Act to the financing of television ads in Wisconsin.

Through 2006, the League continued to support meaningful campaign finance reform, urging Representatives to vote for a ban on leadership PACs as well as support a bill that would close soft money loopholes.

During the 2008 presidential campaign, the League pressed all the candidates to support reform of the presidential public financing system.

In 2007 and 2008, the League endorsed legislation to fix the public financing system for president and to establish congressional public financing for the first time. The League also supported banning leadership PACs and continued to press the courts to properly interpret and enforce campaign finance law.

In the late 2000s, the LWVUS was involved as a "friend of the court" in two pivotal U.S. Supreme Court cases: *Caperton v. Massey* and *Citizens United v. FEC*. In the latter case, the League argued that corporate spending in elections should not be equated with the First Amendment rights of individual citizens.

In 2010, the League reacted swiftly and strongly against the Supreme Court's decision in *Citizens United v. FEC*. The

League president testified before the relevant House committee on the key steps that can be taken to respond, focusing on the importance of including tighter disclosure requirements before the 2010 elections. The League continues to urge passage of the DISCLOSE Act to counter the Court's decision.

In early 2012, the LWVUS Board appointed a Campaign Finance Task force to examine legislative and constitutional efforts to achieve campaign finance reform. Convention 2012 reaffirmed the League's commitment to campaign finance reform by passing a resolution that called for advocating strongly for campaign finance measures including but not limited to constitutional amendments.

In the summer of 2012, the League ran radio ads in Tennessee and Maine asking Senators Corker, Alexander, Snowe and Collins to support campaign finance reform. The ads were timed in anticipation of Congressional action on the DISCLOSE Act. The ads garnered press coverage from outlets in both states.

In the 2012 elections, huge amounts of campaign spending came from so-called independent groups, much of it from secret contributions. The League took on these issues, arguing that much of the "independent" spending was actually coordinated with candidate campaigns, and therefore illegal. The League also pointed to the secret "dark money' and pushed for enhanced disclosure. Also, the League continues to push for legislation to protect and reinvigorate the public financing system for president. In addition, the League continues to work to reinvigorate the dysfunctional Federal Election Commission (FEC) which has refused to enforce the law.

The 2014-2016 National Program on Key Structures of Democracy focused increased attention at every level of League on Money in Politics and included a new study to provide additional detail to the League's position.

Based on the new position statement and previous action on campaign finance reform, the four major elements of the League's MIP plan focus on: disclosure, stopping super PACs (a political committee that can solicit and spend unlimited sums of money. to campaign for or against political

figures), public financing for congressional and presidential elections and reform of the FEC in order to create an effective enforcement agency.

THE LEAGUE'S POSITION

The League of Women Voters believes that the methods of financing political campaigns should:

- **Enhance political equality for all citizens.**
- **Ensure maximum participation by citizens in the political process; protect representative democracy from being distorted by big spending in election campaigns.**
- **Provide voters sufficient information about candidates and campaign issues to make informed choices; ensure transparency and the public's right to know who is using money to influence elections.**
- **Enable candidates to compete equitably for public office; ensure that candidates have sufficient funds to communicate their messages to the public; and combat corruption and undue influence in government.**

The League believes that political corruption includes the following:

- **A candidate or officeholder agrees to vote or work in favor of a donor's interests in exchange for a campaign contribution.**
- **An officeholder or staff gives greater access to donors.**
- **An officeholder votes or works to support policies that reflect the preferences of individuals or organizations in order to attract contributions from them.**
- **A candidate or office holder seeks political contributions implying that there will be retribution unless a donation is given.**
- **The results of the political process consistently favor the interests of significant campaign contributors.**

In order to achieve the goals for campaign finance regulation, the League supports:

- Public financing of elections, either voluntary or mandatory, in which candidates must abide by reasonable spending limits.
- Enhanced enforcement of campaign finance laws that includes changes to ensure that regulatory agencies are properly funded, staffed, and structured to avoid partisan deadlock in the decision-making process.
- Abolishing Super PACs and abolishing spending coordinated or directed by candidates (other than a candidate's own campaign committee)
- Restrictions on direct donations and bundling by lobbyists, which may include monetary limits as well as other regulations.

Until full public financing of elections is enacted, limits on election spending are needed in order to meet the League's goals for protecting democratic processes. Among the different entities that spend money to influence elections, the League supports the following comparative limits:

- Higher spending limits for political parties, genuinely non-partisan voter registration and get-out-the-vote organizations and activities, and candidates' spending money raised from contributors
- Mid-level spending limits for individual citizens (including wealthy individuals), Political Action Committees (with funds contributed by individuals associated with the sponsoring organization, such as employees, stockholders, members and volunteers), and candidates spending their own money
- Lower spending limits for trade associations, labor unions and non-profit organizations from their general treasury funds
- Severely restricted spending by for-profit organizations spending from their corporate treasury funds
- No limits on spending by bona fide newspapers, television, and other media, including the Internet, except to address partisan abuse or use of the media to evade campaign finance regulations

This position is applicable to all federal campaigns for public office: presidential and congressional, primaries as well as general elections. It also may be applied to state and local campaigns.

Statement of Position on Campaign Finance, as Announced by National Board, April 2016.

Selection of the President

A League study of the presidential electoral process culminated in a 1970 position supporting direct election of the President by popular vote as essential to representative government. The League testified and lobbied for legislation to amend the Constitution to replace the Electoral College with direct election of the President, including provisions for a national runoff election in the event no candidates (President or Vice-President) received 40 percent of the vote. The measure, which passed the House and nearly passed the Senate in 1971, has been revived in each Congress without success. In 1997, the LWVUS again called for abolition of the Electoral College and for direct election of the President and Vice-President in testimony before the House Subcommittee on the Constitution.

The League has supported national voting qualifications and procedures for presidential elections to ensure equity for voters from all states and to facilitate the electoral process.

In February 2001, a memo was sent to the state and local Leagues outlining the League's position on the Electoral College under the LWVUS position on Selection of the President.

The League believes strongly that the Electoral College should be abolished and not merely "reformed." One "reform" which the League specifically rejects is the voting by electors based on proportional representation in lieu of the present "winner-takes-all" method. Such a system would apportion the electoral votes of a state based on the popular vote in that state. Instead of making the Electoral College more representative, such proportional voting would increase the chance that no candidate would receive a majority in the Electoral College, thereby sending the election of the President to the House of Representatives where each state, regardless of population, would receive only one vote. Election of the President by the House further removes the decision from the people and is contrary to the "one person, one vote" principle. The League also does not support reform of the Electoral College on a state-by-state basis because the League believes there should be uniformity across the nation in the systems used to elect the President.

The 2002 Convention voted to expand and update the position. The League came to concurrence on a new position in June 2004, which takes into account the entire presidential selection process and supports a process that produces the best possible candidates, informed voters and optimum voter participation.

The 2008 Convention voted to conduct a study of the National Popular Vote proposal, which would establish the popular election of the President through a compact among the states governing how they would cast their votes in the Electoral College. The 2010 Convention adopted a concurrence to support the National Popular Vote compact as another method of selecting the President until such time as the Electoral College is abolished.

THE LEAGUE'S POSITION

The League of Women Voters believes that the direct-popular-vote method for electing the President and Vice-President is essential to representative government. The League of Women Voters believes, therefore, that the Electoral College should be abolished. We support the use of the National Popular Vote Compact as one acceptable way to achieve the goal of the direct popular vote for election of the president until the abolition of the Electoral College is accomplished. The League also supports uniform voting qualifications and procedures for presidential elections. The League supports changes in the presidential election system from the candidate selection process to the general election. We support efforts to provide voters with sufficient information about candidates and their positions, public policy issues and the selection process itself. The League supports action to ensure that the media, political parties, candidates, and all levels of government achieve these goals and provide that information.

Statement of Position on Selection of the President, as Announced by National Board, January 1970, Revised March 1982, Updated June 2004 and Revised by the 2010 Convention.

CITIZEN RIGHTS

Citizen's Right to Know/Citizen Participation

The League has long worked for the citizen's right to know and for broad citizen participation in government. League support for open meetings was first made explicit in the 1972 Congress position. In 1973, Leagues were empowered to apply that position at the state and local levels. In 1974, the Convention added to the League Principles the requisite that "government bodies protect the citizen's right to know by giving adequate notice of proposed actions, holding open meetings and making public records accessible," and decided that Leagues could act on the Principles, with the necessary safeguards of member understanding and support. The League supported the 1976 Government in the Sunshine law to enhance citizens' access to information.

In the 1980s, the League monitored and lobbied to revamp the way federal rules and regulations are made. The League supports broad public participation at every stage of the rule-making process.

The LWVUS, in coalition with numerous other organizations, opposed efforts in 1983 by the Office of Management and Budget (OMB) to restrict the political advocacy activities of nonprofit organizations and thereby limit citizen participation in federal policy making. The coalition's opposition resulted in a much less onerous OMB regulation.

As part of its concerns about citizen rights, the League supports lobbying disclosure reform to provide information on the pressures exerted on the national policy-making process and guarantee citizen access to influence the process.

Early in 1995, as part of the Contract with America, the congressional leadership launched a broad attack on citizen participation in government decision making. Under the guise of "regulatory reform," bills were introduced to make it much more difficult for federal agencies to promulgate regulations dealing with health, safety and the environment. These bills were based on the premise that regulations should be judged solely on their cost to the public and private sectors, and not on their benefits to society.

The League responded quickly to this major threat, lobbying both houses of Congress in opposition. Along with members of 200 other consumers, environmental and disability rights organizations, League members met with their members of Congress and participated in media activities opposing these efforts. The opposition succeeded in stalling all regulatory reform legislation in the Senate in 1996.

The League also responded to a major congressional attack in the 104th Congress, when an amendment to severely limit the ability of nonprofits to speak out on public policy matters was added to several 1996 appropriations bills. Known as the Istook amendment after its primary sponsor, Rep. Ernest Istook (R-OK), the amendment was designed to limit citizen participation by forcing nonprofits to choose between community service and public policy.

The League, with hundreds of other nonprofits, organized a massive campaign to educate the public and members of Congress about the serious implications of this legislation. The Istook amendment eventually was dropped from the appropriations bills, but similar efforts continued in the 104th and 105th Congresses. The League continues to monitor attempts to gag nonprofit organizations.

In June 2000, the LWVUS urged the Federal Communications Commission (FCC) to issue requirements for broadcasters to cover local public affairs.

Beginning with a grant from the Open Society Institute in 2001, the LWVEF has participated in the Judicial Independence project. State and local Leagues, working in conjunction with the national office, assess the levels of judicial independence in their state and develop citizen education campaigns to educate their communities about this important issue. A key part of this program is encouraging Leagues to include judicial candidates in their voter guides and to organize candidate forums for judicial candidates. In 2002 and 2003, more than 200 Leagues nationwide organized 70 forums, meetings and workshops spotlighting their state court systems and the value of an independent judiciary.

This project continued in 2004-2008 and evolved into Safeguarding U.S. Democracy: Promoting an Independent Judiciary, a program to increase citizen understanding of the importance of our nation's system of separation of powers and highlight the vital need for protecting a vibrant and independent judiciary. In 2009 and 2010, the project gained a new focus on promoting diversity at all levels of the state judiciary. In the first year of The Quest for a More Diverse Judiciary project, the Leagues in Kansas worked on this initiative and saw success in the new appointments that followed. In the second year, South Carolina was added and was very successful. In 2012, the State of Washington was added with a more limited scope and in the same year the League published "From Theory to Practice: A Grassroots Education Campaign," a practical guide for those wishing to created state-wide education campaigns and illustrating each step of the campaign with practical information learned in Kansas, South Carolina and Washington.

In 2002 and 2004, the LWVUS participated as *amicus curiae* in the case of *Miller-El v. Cockrell*. The League's interest in the case focused on the use of race-based peremptory challenges to jurors as a means to block citizen participation in government. The Supreme Court agreed with the League's position, but a lower federal court failed to carry out this interpretation and the case was once again before the Supreme Court in late 2004.

In the 109th Congress, the LWVUS endorsed the Openness Promotes Effectiveness in our National Government (OPEN) Act which expands the accessibility and accountability of the federal government by strengthening the Freedom of Information Act and making information more readily available to the public.

The LWVEF has engaged in a number of efforts to assist Leagues in this area, and also to become more visible in federal transparency efforts. In 2005, the League launched an Openness in Government: Looking for the Sunshine, a project to broaden public awareness about the issues involved in, and the threats related to, accountability and transparency in government. The League developed educational materials about federal, state and local laws concerning citizen access, the extent and types of threats to these laws that have occurred in recent years, and data on the increasing levels of information being put off-limits since 9-11. The project was continued in 2006, under the name Observing Your Government in Action: Protecting Your Right to Know.

Additional projects were initiated in the following years. One focused on public document audits, providing financial support to Leagues in 11 states and a toolkit, "Surveying Public Documents: Protecting Your Right to Know." In 2010, work started on an online resource called "Sunshine 2.0," which will provide criteria for assessing the transparency of local government websites and other online technologies.

At the federal level, the League has been active in providing advice to the Obama Administration as it implemented its Openness in Government Directive. In so doing, we have also helped a number of good government groups work together.

The League has served as a cosponsor of the annual Sunshine Week since 2006, taking part in kickoff events in Washington, DC. Sunshine Week sponsors a nationwide live webcast to stimulate public discussion about why open government is important to everyone and why it is under challenge today. Leagues are encouraged to participate.

THE LEAGUE'S POSITION
The League of Women Voters believes that democratic government depends upon informed and active participation at all levels of government. The League further believes that governmental bodies must protect the citizen's right to know by giving adequate notice of proposed actions, holding open meetings and making public records accessible.

Statement of Position on the Citizen's Right to Know/Citizen Participation, as Announced by National Board, June 1984.

Individual Liberties

Individual liberties, a long-standing League Principle, have been central for the League during times of national tension.

The "witch hunt" period of the early 1950s led the League to undertake a two-year Freedom Agenda community education program on issues such as freedom of speech. Next, a focused study on the federal loyalty/security programs culminated in a position that emphasized protection of individual rights.

The 1976 Convention incorporated the League's individual liberties Principle into the national Program, thus authorizing the League to act against major threats to basic constitutional rights. Subsequent Conventions reaffirmed that commitment, and in 1982 the LWVUS Board authorized a specific position statement on individual liberties.

In 2003, the League contacted members of both houses to express concern about several far-reaching provisions of the USA PATRIOT Act, passed in October 2001, asking members of Congress to scale back some of them. The League lobbied on behalf of the bipartisan Security and Freedom Ensured (SAFE) Act in 2004, which addresses many of the PATRIOT Act's problems, while still allowing law enforcement officials broad authority to combat terrorism.

Late in the 108th Congress, the League lobbied against the House version of legislation to overhaul the organization of U.S. intelligence operations because it went beyond the scope of the September 11th Commission's recommendations, expanding the government's investigative and prosecutorial powers and infringing upon civil liberties. When the bill was passed, as the National Intelligence Reform Act, in December 2004, it had been amended and a number of the troubling provisions that the League opposed were eliminated.

At the 2004 Convention, League delegates voted to make civil liberties a top priority in the next biennium. The LWVUS appointed an Advisory Task Force and created an online discussion list to foster dialogue about the League's course of action.

In 2005, the LWVUS also expressed concerns about reports of torture by the United States military and actively supported the "McCain amendment," banning cruel, inhuman or degrading treatment or punishment of anyone under custody or control of the U.S. armed forces. The amendment passed as part of the Department of Defense appropriation.

During the 109th Congress, the League continued to lobby in support of the SAFE Act and in opposition to the pending reauthorization of specific provisions of the USA PATRIOT Act. While final reauthorization did not address many of our concerns, there was limited improvement in some critical provisions.

In 2005, the LWVEF sponsored a nationwide project, Local Voices: Citizen Conversations on Civil Liberties and Secure Communities, to foster public dialogue about the balance between civil liberties and homeland security. The League sponsored public discussions in ten ethnically, economically and geographically diverse cities. It released the findings of these discussions and public opinion research on the issue at the U.S. Capitol in September 2005.

In 2007-2008, the League fought legislation in both houses that continued allowing the Executive branch to conduct warrantless wiretapping without judicial review, and supported legislation that would protect personal information of citizens and limit the FBI's authority to issue national security letters in lieu of judicial warrants to produce information and materials.

In 2009, the League joined other organizations in support of the JUSTICE (Judiciously Using Surveillance Tools In Counterterrorism Efforts) Act, legislation to amend expiring provisions of the US PATRIOT Act.

THE LEAGUE'S POSITION
The League of Women Voters believes in the individual liberties guaranteed by the Constitution of the United States. The League is convinced that individual rights now protected by the Constitution should not be weakened or abridged.

Statement of Position on Individual Liberties, as Announced by National Board, March 1982.

Constitutional Amendment Proposals

Following the January 2016 meeting, the League of Women Voters board announced a new position outlining considerations for evaluating constitutional amendment proposals. State Leagues can use this new position, as well as the new position calling for safeguards to govern the constitutional convention process, to address the ongoing debates in many legislatures regarding constitutional conventions, in particular as they related to the Balanced Budget amendment.

THE LEAGUE'S POSITION
The League of Women Voters will only support a proposed amendment to the U.S. Constitution if it advances and conforms to a LWVUS position.

In addition, the League believes the following should be considered in identifying an appropriate and well-crafted constitutional amendment:

- **Whether the public policy objective addresses matters of such acute and abiding importance that the fundamental charter of our nation must be changed. Amendments are changes to a document that provides stability to our system and should be undertaken to address extreme problems or long-term needs.**
- **Whether the amendment as written would be effective in achieving its policy objective. Amendments that may be unenforceable, miss the objective, or have unintended consequences may not achieve the policy objective.**

- Whether the amendment would either make our political system more democratic or protect individual rights. Most adopted amendments have sought to make our system more representative or to protect the rights of minorities.
- Whether the public policy objective can be achieved by a legislative or political approach that is less difficult than a constitutional amendment. In order to expend resources wisely, it is important to consider whether legislation or political action is more likely to succeed than an amendment.
- Whether the public policy objective is more suited to a constitutional and general approach than to a statutory and detailed approach. It is important to consider whether the goal can best be achieved by an overall value statement, which will be interpreted by the courts, or with specific statutory detail to resolve important issues and reduce ambiguity.

Statement of Position on Evaluating Constitutional Amendment Proposals, as Announced by National Board, January 2016.

Constitutional Conventions

Following the January 2016 meeting, the League of Women Voters board announced a new position calling for safeguards to govern the constitutional convention process under Article V of the U.S. Constitution. State Leagues can use this new position, as well as the new position outlining considerations for evaluating constitutional amendment proposals, to address the ongoing debates in many legislatures regarding constitutional conventions, in particular as they related to the Balanced Budget amendment.

THE LEAGUE'S POSITION
The League of Women Voters is concerned that there are many unresolved questions about the powers and processes of an Article V Constitutional Convention. The League believes that such a convention should be called only if the following conditions are in place:

- The Constitutional Convention must be transparent and not conducted in secret. The public has a right to know what is being debated and voted on.
- Representation at the Constitutional Convention must be based on population rather than one state, one vote, and delegates should be elected rather than appointed. The delegates represent citizens, should be elected by them, and must be distributed by U.S. population.
- Voting at the Constitutional Convention must be by delegate, not by state. Delegates from one state can have varying views and should be able to express them by individual votes.
- The Constitutional Convention must be limited to a specific topic. It is important to guard against a "runaway convention" which considers multiple issues or topics that were not initiated by the states.
- Only state resolutions on a single topic count when determining if a Constitutional Convention should be called. Counting state requests by topic ensures that there is sufficient interest in a particular subject to call a Convention and enhances citizen interest and participation in the process.
- The validity of state calls for an Article V Constitutional Convention must be determined by the most recent action of the state. If a state has enacted a rescission of its call, that rescission must be respected by Congress.

Statement of Position on Constitutional Conventions under Article V of the U.S. Constitution as Announced by National Board, January 2016.

Public Policy on Reproductive Choices

The 1982 Convention voted to develop a League position on Public Policy on Reproductive Choices through concurrence. That fall, League members studied the issue and agreed to concur with a statement derived from positions reached by the New Jersey and Massachusetts Leagues. The LWVUS announced the position in January 1983.

In 1983, the LWVUS successfully pressed for defeat of S.J. Res. 3, a proposed constitutional amendment that would have overturned *Roe v. Wade*, the landmark Supreme Court decision that the right of privacy includes the right of a woman, in consultation with her doctor, to decide to terminate a pregnancy. The League joined as an *amicus* in two successful lawsuits challenging proposed regulations by the federal Department of Health and Human Services (HHS), thus thwarting attempts to implement regulations requiring parental notification by federally funded family planning centers that provide prescription contraceptives to teenagers.

The League has joined with other pro-choice organizations in continuous opposition to restrictions on the right of privacy in reproductive choices that have appeared in Congress as legislative riders to funding measures. In 1985, the League joined as an *amicus* in a lawsuit challenging a Pennsylvania law intended to deter women from having abortions. In 1986, the Supreme Court found the law unconstitutional, upholding a woman's right to make reproductive choices.

In 1986, the League opposed congressional provisions to revoke the tax-exempt status of any organization that performs, finances or provides facilities for any abortion not necessary to save the life of a pregnant woman. In 1987, the League unsuccessfully opposed regulations governing Title X of the Public Health Service Act. The League reaffirmed that individuals have the right to make their own reproductive choices, consistent with the constitutional right of privacy, stating that the proposed rule violated this right by prohibiting counseling and referral for abortion services by clinics receiving Title X funds.

In 1988 and 1990, the League urged congressional committees to report an appropriations bill for the District of Columbia without amendments limiting abortion funding. The League also supported 1988 legislation that would have restored Medicaid funding for abortions in cases of rape or incest.

The League joined an *amicus* brief to uphold a woman's right of privacy to make reproductive choices in *Webster v. Reproductive Health Services*. In July 1989, a sharply divided Supreme Court issued a decision that severely eroded a woman's right of privacy to choose abortion. Although

Webster did not deny the constitutional right to choose abortion, it effectively overruled a significant portion of the 1973 *Roe* decision by upholding a Missouri statute that prohibited the use of public facilities, employees or funds for counseling, advising or performing abortions and required doctors to conduct viability tests on fetuses 20 weeks or older before aborting them.

The League supported the March for Women's Lives in 1989. Also, the League joined an *amicus* brief in *Turnock v. Ragsdale*, challenging an Illinois statute that would have effectively restricted access to abortions, including those in the first trimester, by providing strict requirements for abortion clinics.

In 1990, the LWVUS joined the national Pro-Choice Coalition and began work in support of the Freedom of Choice Act, designed to place into federal law the principles of *Roe v. Wade.*

In 1990-91, the League, in *New York v. Sullivan,* opposed the HHS "gag rule" regulations that prohibit abortion information, services or referrals by family-planning programs receiving Title X public health funds. The Supreme Court upheld the regulations, Leagues nationwide responded in opposition, and the LWVUS urged Congress to overturn the gag rule.

The 1990 League Convention voted to work on issues dealing with the right of privacy in reproductive choices, domestic and international family planning and reproductive health care, and initiatives to decrease teen pregnancy and infant mortality (based on the International Relations and Social Policy positions). The LWVUS acted on a series of pro-choice legislative initiatives. It supported the International Family Planning Act, which would have reversed U.S. policy denying family planning funds to foreign organizations that provide abortion services or information. It opposed the Department of Defense policy prohibiting military personnel from obtaining abortions at military hospitals overseas and supported the right of the District of Columbia to use its own revenues to provide Medicaid abortions for low income women.

In 1991 and 1992, the League continued to fight efforts to erode the constitutional right of reproductive choice by supporting the Freedom of Choice Act and attempts to overturn the gag rule. In coalition with 178 other groups, the League filed an *amicus* brief in *Planned Parenthood of Southeastern Pennsylvania v. Casey*, arguing that constitutional rights, once recognized, should not be snatched away. In June 1992, the Court decision partially upheld the Pennsylvania regulations, seriously undermining the principles of *Roe*. In response, Leagues stepped up lobbying efforts for the Freedom of Choice Act. The 1992 LWVUS Convention voted to continue work on all domestic and international aspects of reproductive choice.

In 1993, the League continued to support legislative attempts to overturn the gag rule. In late 1993, President Clinton signed an executive order overturning it and other restrictive anti-choice policies. The LWVUS continued to work for passage of the Freedom of Choice Act and against the Hyde Amendment. The LWVUS supported the Freedom of Access to Clinic Entrances (FACE) Act, a response to escalating violence at abortion clinics. The FACE bill passed and was signed by the President in 1993.

During the 1993-1994 health care debate, the League pressed for inclusion of reproductive services, including abortion, in any health care reform package. In 1995, the League again opposed amendments denying Medicaid funding for abortions for victims of rape and incest.

In 1998, the LWVUS opposed the Child Custody Protection Act, federal legislation designed to make it illegal for an adult other than a parent to assist a minor in obtaining an out-of-state abortion.

In spring 2000, the LWVUS joined an *amicus* brief in *Stenberg v. Carhart*, urging the Supreme Court to affirm a U.S. Court of Appeals ruling that a Nebraska law criminalizing commonly used abortion procedures was unconstitutional. The Court's affirmation of the ruling in June 2000 was pivotal in further defining a woman's right to reproductive freedom.

As Congress continued to threaten reproductive rights with legislative riders to appropriations bills, the League lobbied Congress in opposition to these back door attempts to limit reproductive choice.

In 2002, the LWVUS lobbied extensively against attempts to limit funding for family planning and, in 2003, the League lobbied the House to support funding for the United Nations Population Fund, which lost by just one vote. The League strongly opposed the passage of the so-called Partial-Birth Abortion Act in 2003, but it was passed and signed into law.

In March 2004, the LWVUS lobbied in opposition to the Unborn Victims of Violence Act (UVVA), which conveys legal status under the Federal Criminal code to an embryo and fetus, but Congress passed the bill and the president signed it.

The League cosponsored the March for Women's Lives in Washington, DC, on April 25, 2004, which demonstrated and drew widespread support for the right to make reproductive choices, including many state and local League delegations.

In 2008, the League filed official comments with the HHS, voicing concern over "conscience" regulations that would limit reproductive health care options for women by allowing physicians, pharmacists and other providers to sharply limit their services according to their own views on reproductive health care.

In 2009, the League joined other groups urging rescission of the "conscience" regulations. The HHS subsequently modified the regulations to preserve women's reproductive health care and the doctor-patient relationship.

In 2012, the League responded to attempts to allow any employer or provider who claimed an ill-defined "religious or moral" objection to a health care service, such as reproductive health care, to be exempted from providing such coverage under the Affordable Care Act (ACA). The League opposed this exemption which would undermine the very premise of the ACA that all persons, regardless of gender, should be eligible for health services under the ACA, and that failure to do so is discrimination based on sex.

The League also lobbied Congress in support of fully funding the Title X Family Planning program in response to proposed cuts to Title X, which has provided family planning and reproductive health care services to millions of low-income individuals and families.

In 2013, the LWVUS submitted comments opposing religious exemptions for contraceptive services. This debate continued in the courts and the League joined with other concerned organizations in opposing broad "religious exemptions" to the requirement that all insurance plans provide access to contraception as basic care in the Supreme Court case of *Burwell v. Hobby Lobby Stores.*

THE LEAGUE'S POSITION
The League of Women Voters believes public policy in a pluralistic society must affirm the constitutional right of privacy of the individual to make reproductive choices.

Statement of Position on Public Policy on Reproductive Choices, as Announced by National Board, January 1983.

CONGRESS AND THE PRESIDENCY

Congress

Congress has been a part of the League agenda for many years. In 1944, the League adopted as a Program focus: "Strengthening governmental procedures to improve the legislative process and relationship between Congress and the Executive." In 1946, the LWVUS worked successfully for passage of the Legislative Reorganization Act. In 1954, the League unsuccessfully called on Congress to coordinate and simplify its budgetary procedures.

In 1970, the League undertook a comprehensive study of Congress, leading to a 1972 position on specific changes to make Congress more responsive to citizen needs. League members urged Congress to open the doors to its committee and hearing rooms, free up access to leadership positions and coordinate its budgetary processes.

League support of procedural changes and the 1974 Budget Reform and Impoundment Control Act led to many improvements:

- New committee procedures that modified the seniority system and made committee membership more representative of diverse interests
- Rule changes for more adequate staffing
- Electronic voting
- Modification of the Senate cloture rule
- Moves to open all committee meetings and proceedings to the public, except when matters of national security are involved
- Reorganization of the budget process, so that Congress can establish priorities and evaluate the budget package as a whole

The League has continued to assess proposals for additional procedural changes in Congress. In 1986, the League urged the Senate to provide for radio broadcast and trial closed-circuit television coverage. In 1989, the LWVUS successfully urged the House to enact an ethics reform package that included limits on honoraria and outside income. In 1998, the League joined 13 national groups in urging the Senate Majority Leader to eliminate the use of "secret holds" in the Senate. The League and 52 other groups endorsed draft legislation to put Congressional Research Service reports and products on the Internet.

In 1991, the League announced its opposition to term limits for members of the U.S. Congress on the grounds that such limits would adversely affect the accountability, representativeness and effective performance of Congress, and, by decreasing the power of Congress, would upset the balance of power between Congress and an already powerful presidency. The 1992 LWVUS Convention reaffirmed opposition to term limits and authorized state and local Leagues to use national positions to take action on term limits for state and local offices.

In 1993-1994, the Leagues of Washington and Arkansas participated in suits challenging state term limits laws based on the U.S. Constitution. In 1995, after hearing the Arkansas case, the Supreme Court agreed that term limits imposed by states on the U.S. House and Senate are unconstitutional. Proposals to amend the Constitution to allow or set federal term limits failed to receive the necessary two-thirds majority in both houses. The League vigorously opposed the proposed amendment through testimony, lobbying and grassroots action. In 1997, the League again successfully lobbied House members on this issue.

In 1999, the LWVUS and the LWV of Missouri filed an *amicus* brief in the U.S. Court of Appeals in *Cook v. Gralike*, challenging a Missouri law requiring the phrase "disregarded voters' instruction on term limits" to appear on the ballot next to any candidate's name who had not taken certain actions related to term limits. The law was struck down by the Appeals Court, both because it was a backdoor attempt to impose term limits and because it burdened the election process. The state League and the LWVUS subsequently filed *amicus* briefs with the Supreme Court while the case was considered on appeal.

In 2007 and 2008, the League responded directly to congressional scandals that demonstrated a failure in the mechanisms that regulated ethics and lobbying. The League pushed Congress to enact lobbying reform measures: to set fundraising limits on lobbyists and lobbying firms; change the gift, travel and employment relationships among Members of Congress, lobbyists and lobbying firms; and institute new and effective enforcement mechanisms.

In 2008, the House passed new ethics procedures, including new ethics rules, disclosure requirements for campaign contributions "bundled" by lobbyists, and a new ethics enforcement process. The League also supported strengthening the investigative powers of the new Office of Congressional Ethics by providing access to subpoena power so investigators would be able to compel cooperation from outside entities and individuals, congressional staff and Members.

In 2010 and again in 2012 and 2014, the League and coalition partners sent a letter to the Speaker urging him to preserve and strengthen House ethics rules and standards of conduct.

THE LEAGUE'S POSITION

The League of Women Voters believes that structures and practices of the U.S. Congress must be characterized by openness, accountability, representativeness, decision making capability and effective performance. Responsive legislative processes must meet these criteria:

ACCOUNTABILITY - A Congress responsive to citizens and able to hold its own leaders, committees and members responsible for their actions and decisions

REPRESENTATIVENESS - A Congress whose leaders, committees and members represent the nation as a whole, as well as their own districts and states

DECISION MAKING CAPABILITY - A Congress with the knowledge, resources and power to make decisions that meet national needs and reconcile conflicting interests and priorities

EFFECTIVE PERFORMANCE - A Congress able to function in an efficient manner with a minimum of conflict, wasted time and duplication of effort

OPEN GOVERNMENT - A Congress whose proceedings in committee as well as on the floor are open to the fullest extent possible.

Statement of Position on Congress, as Announced by National Board, April 1972 and Revised March 1982.

The Presidency

In view of growing public concern about presidential powers, the 1974 Convention adopted a two-year study of the executive branch with emphasis on presidential powers, succession and tenure. The 1976 position tied closely to earlier positions on Congress and enabled the League to take action to promote a dynamic balance between the powers of the President and those of Congress. Such a balance, according to member agreement, requires elimination of unnecessary secrecy between the branches, periodic congressional reviews of executive agreements and states of national emergency, and proper use of the procedures spelled out in the War Powers Resolution. LWVUS support of anti-impoundment measures in 1973 also was consistent with the emphasis on the balance of power between the two branches.

In 1985, the League opposed the Gramm-Rudman-Hollings Balanced Budget and Emergency Deficit Control Act as a threat to this balance of power. In 1986, the Supreme Court declared unconstitutional the key part of the law that provided for automatic budget cuts to be decided by the Comptroller General if deficit targets were missed. A revision of the law met the separation-of-powers objection of the Court.

THE LEAGUE'S POSITION

The League of Women Voters believes that presidential power should be exercised within the constitutional framework of a dynamic balance between the executive and legislative branches. Accountability and responsibility to the people require that unnecessary secrecy between the President and Congress be eliminated. Therefore, the League supports the following measures:

EXECUTIVE AGREEMENTS - **Presidential authority to negotiate international executive agreements should be preserved. Accountability to the public requires that the President report to Congress the text of all such agreements and that Congress review them periodically.**

WAR POWERS - **The President should be required to seek the advice of the Congress before introducing U.S. armed forces into situations where hostilities are imminent, to report promptly to Congress any action taken, and to obtain within a specified time congressional approval for continued military activity.**

EMERGENCY POWERS - **Presidential authority to declare a state of national emergency should be subject to periodic congressional review. The President should transmit to Congress yearly notice of all existing national emergencies and significant orders issued under each. Congress should review the emergencies and significant orders issued under each. Congress should review the emergencies every six months and should have the power to terminate them at any time by concurrent resolution. All states of emergency now in existence should be terminated after a grace period for adjustment.**

FISCAL POWERS - **The President should exercise executive responsibility for sound management of public funds in a manner consistent with the programs and priorities established by Congress. This requires procedures for congressional consideration of the budget as a whole and measures for congressional disapproval of presidential impoundment of funds.**

SUCCESSION AND TENURE - **The League of Women Voters of the United States supports the succession procedures spelled out in the 25th Amendment. However, the League favors a limit on the amount of time Congress may take to confirm the Vice-President. The League also favors retention of a two-term limitation on presidential terms of office.**

Statement of Position on the Presidency, as Announced by National Board, January 1976 and Revised March 1982.

PRIVATIZATION

Convention 2010 delegates voted to undertake a study of the issue of Privatization. Local and state Leagues across the country participated in the study and a position was announced in June 2012.

THE LEAGUE'S POSITION

The League of Women Voters believes that when governmental entities consider the transfer of governmental services, assets and/or functions to the private sector, the community impact and goals of such transfers must be identified and considered. Further, the League believes that transparency, accountability, and preservation of the common good must be ensured.

The League believes that some government provided services could be delivered more efficiently by private entities; however, privatization is not appropriate in all circumstances. Privatization is not appropriate when the provision of services by the government is necessary to preserve the common good, to protect national or local security or to meet the needs of the most vulnerable members of society. While the League recognizes that the definition of core government services will vary by level of government and community values, services fundamental to the governance of a democratic society should not be privatized in their entirety. These services include the electoral process, justice system, military, public safety, public health, education, transportation, environmental protection and programs that protect and provide basic human needs.

The decision to privatize a public service should be made after an informed, transparent planning process and thorough analysis of the implications of privatizing service delivery. While specific criteria will vary by service and local conditions, the League believes the following considerations apply to most decisions to transfer public services, assets and functions to the private sector:

- On-going and timely communication with stakeholders and the public
- Statement of the circumstances as they exist and what is to be gained
- Definition of the quality, level and cost of service expected
- Assessment of the private market; whether there are providers to assure competitive pricing and delivery recognizing that in some cases, there may not be multiple providers if a service is specialized (e.g., high tech, airports)
- Cost-benefit analyses evaluating short and long term costs of privatization, including the ongoing costs of contract administration and oversight
- An understanding of the impact on customers, the broader community, environment and public employees
- An open, competitive bidding process with clearly defined criteria to be used in selecting a contractor
- A provision and process to ensure the services or assets will be returned to the government if a contractor fails to perform
- A data-driven selection of private entities whose goals, purposes, and means are not incompatible with the public well-being
- The careful negotiation and drafting of the controlling privatization contract
- Adequate oversight and periodic performance monitoring of the privatized services by the government entity to ensure that the private entity is complying with all relevant laws and regulations, contract terms and conditions, and ethical standards, including public disclosure and comment.

The League believes that the enactment of state laws and issuance of regulations to control the process and delivery of privatization within a state's jurisdiction is often appropriate and desirable. Best practices for government regulation of the privatization process should include the following requirements:

- An open process that allows for citizen input and oversight in a timely manner
- A reasonable feasibility study and project evaluation appropriate to the size and scope of the project
- The establishment of carefully crafted criteria for selection of the private-entity (beyond the lowest cost bid)
- Additional consideration for local bidders in order to support the local economy
- The retention of liability and responsibility with the government entity
- Allowance for and promotion of opportunities for innovation and collaboration

- Provision for employment, benefits and training plans on behalf of employees displaced as a result of privatization.

Statement of Position on Privatization as announced by the National Board in June 2012.

INTERNATIONAL RELATIONS

Promote peace in an interdependent world by working cooperatively with other nations and strengthening international organizations.

A commitment to international cooperation as an essential path to world peace is deeply rooted in League history. Founded just after World War I, the League rejected a policy of isolationism as "neither wise nor possible for this nation." The League's commitment has taken many forms. Action to support free trade began during the Depression and support for aid to developing countries in the 1950s. As World War II ended, the League launched a nationwide campaign to build public understanding of the agreements setting up the United Nations and was proud to be one of the nongovernmental organizations first affiliated with the UN, a relationship that continues to this day.

In the 1960s, the League played an important role in educating citizens and creating the climate for normalization of U.S. relations with the People's Republic of China. Also in the 1960s, after a reappraisal of trade policy, the League took action to reduce trade barriers while supporting assistance for economic adjustment in the United States. Throughout the 1970s, the League was active on trade issues, working for the history-making multilateral process that built a new structure for international trade.

In the 1980s, positions on Arms Control and on Military Policy and Defense Spending added new dimensions to the League's international relations efforts. With these positions, the League supported international negotiations and agreements to reduce the risk of war and prevent the development and deployment of nuclear weapons, and worked against the costly, technologically suspect and destabilizing national missile defense program.

Adoption of a U.S. Relations with Developing Countries position in 1986 provided further definition to the League's efforts to promote peace, with special emphasis on human rights, sound management of natural resources and economic development.

In the 1990s, the League launched training and education projects to build political participation in emerging democracies. Beginning in nations from Eastern Europe and the former Soviet Union and extending to Africa and the Americas, the League experience has proved invaluable in developing the potential for citizen participation and nongovernmental organizations (NGOs) in democratic systems, especially for women leaders.

In the 2000s, the League expanded its "global democracy" program and updated its positions on the United Nations and International Trade. The League continued its strong support for the United Nations, added its support for the International Criminal Court and endorsed enhanced peace operations. The League reiterated its support for measures to expand international trade, while recognizing the importance of protecting environmental, labor and political values.

UNITED NATIONS

At the first League Convention in 1920, delegates called for "adhesion of the United States to the League of Nations with least possible delay," in recognition of the need for a mechanism to facilitate settlement of international disputes. When the issue of U.S. participation in the League of Nations turned into a bitter partisan battle, active League support did not materialize until 1932.

During World War II, the League, conscious of its earlier hesitancy, began to study "U.S. participation in the making and execution of plans for worldwide reconstruction and for a postwar organization for peace to eventually include all peoples, regardless of race, religion or political persuasion." In 1944, the League supported "U.S. membership in an international organization for the peaceful settlement of disputes, with the machinery to handle economic, social and political problems."

Even before the United Nations (UN) was formally established, the League launched an unprecedented nationwide campaign to help build public understanding of the Dumbarton Oaks and Bretton Woods agreements to establish the United Nations, the World Bank and the International Monetary Fund. The League trained more than 5,000 speakers and distributed more than a million brochures during a six-month period. At the UN Charter Conference in 1945, the League was one of 42 nongovernmental organizations invited by President Truman to serve as consultants to the U.S. delegation. Since then, the League has maintained a presence at the United Nations through its UN Observers, working with UN agencies, member states and other NGOs to advance LWVUS positions, and by periodically hosting "League Day at the UN" for League members.

The UN position evolved through continued study. By 1948, the League called for strengthening the UN and its specialized agencies through increased use, adequate financial contributions and improved procedures. It also supported the UN's peacekeeping functions. In 1962, the League evaluated "means of strengthening the UN under present conditions," most notably heightened antagonisms between the United States and the Soviet Union.

In 1976, the League reexamined the UN system "with emphasis on relations between developed and developing countries and their implications for U.S. policy." Members studied how world issues had changed alignments at the United Nations from a primarily East-West to an increasingly rich-nation/poor-nation focus and its effect on U.S. participation in the UN system. The result was a resounding reaffirmation of support for a strengthened UN system and agreement that the United States should work constructively within the UN to further our foreign policy goals.

The League consistently monitors U.S. actions at the UN, engaging in programs at the U.S. Mission and providing support for mutually held policies. The League continues to urge adequate funding for the UN, both by regular assessments and voluntary contributions, full payment of U.S. financial obligations to the UN and full U.S. participation in the UN system.

In addition to supporting increased use and strength of the UN peacekeeping machinery, under the UN position in support of "continuing efforts to reduce the risk of war," the League has lobbied for Senate ratification of certain disarmament measures, notably the UN-negotiated nuclear nonproliferation treaty. Leagues' efforts in their communities to develop public understanding and awareness of UN accomplishments, limitations and potential took on special significance in 1995 when the League celebrated its 75th anniversary and the United Nations its 50th.

In 1995, the League participated in the UN 4thWorld Conference on Women and the NGO Forum on Women in Beijing, China, sponsoring workshops on Organizing Candidate Debates and Making Democracy Work: Strategies for Grassroots Organization, Education and Advocacy. This was followed in 1999 with a League co-sponsored regional conference of the President's Interagency Council on Women 2000: Beijing Plus Five, to prepare for the Special Session of the General Assembly on Women 2000: Gender Equality, Development and Peace for the Twenty-First Century, which our UN Observers were accredited to attend in 2000.

In 1997, the League was granted Special Consultative Status with the United Nations Economic and Social Council, which provides the opportunity to make interventions on issues the League supports. We joined other NGOs in submitting an official statement on behalf of the Girl Child that was presented at the UN Commission on the Status of Women meeting in March 2000. As a result of interventions, the League has successfully launched and supported the Working Group on Girls (WGG), a coalition of 80+ NGOs dedicated to focusing governments on the plight of girls throughout the world. The International Day of the Girl is also celebrated around the world as a result of League and WGG efforts. Women in Saudi Arabia enjoy the right to vote after the League provided an intervention that linked women's enfranchisement with GDP.

League activity on women and girl-related issues continued in the 2000s. In 2002, the LWVUS submitted testimony to the Senate Foreign Relations Committee in support of Senate ratification of CEDAW (UN Convention for the Elimination of All Forms of Discrimination Against Women). The League joined other NGOs in official statements to the

UN Commission on the Status of Women: advocating protection of girls' rights in a life cycle approach to gender issues in 2004; emphasizing that financing for girls' equality and for the empowerment of girls is a basic and sound strategy for the implementation of all human rights in 2008. The League also joined the United Nation's Campaign UNITE to End Violence against Women, 2008-2015, whose overall objective is raising public awareness and increasing political will and resources for preventing and responding to all forms of violence against women and girls worldwide. In 2011, as the move to ratify CEDAW continued, the LWVUS submitted testimony to the Senate Judiciary Committee on Civil and Constitutional Rights.

Since then, the League, in coordination with WGG, developed a comprehensive strategy to prevent sexual human trafficking at major events. This strategy to Prevent Violence Against Children was adopted by the Special Representative to the UN Secretary General in her work with member states on preventing violence. Additionally, it was adopted by Brazil and implemented at its 2014 World Cup and Mardi Gras, as well as by the NJ Attorney General for the 2014 Super Bowl. The United States has included components of the strategy in its 2014 Trafficking in Persons Report.

In June 2014, the League formally adopted a position opposing human trafficking. As a result of that position, The LWVUS UN Observers are focusing efforts in the areas of demand and labor trafficking.

In 2002, the League urged President George W. Bush to work with the UN to develop clear policy goals and actions with regard to the U.S.'s possible intervention in Iraq. On initiation of combat operations, the League's Board issued a statement saying that continued diplomatic efforts through the UN would have better served international unity, and military force should have been used as a tool of last resort.

Leagues nationwide work to realize the United Nations' Millennium Goals outlined by UN Secretary General Kofi Annan at the September 2000 Millennium Summit and adopted by 191 states. In 2005, the League urged the Administration to support the goals of the UN's 2005 World Summit Outcome Document, a historic effort to end global poverty, promote peace and strengthen the UN, and urged Congress to reject the United Nations Reform Act.

In 2015, League members had the opportunity to directly voice their opinions and witness UN conferences through the use of technology. By voting on the "Goals We Want," LWV members had an opportunity to encourage the adoption of post-2015 goals seeking to eliminate severe world poverty, encourage mandatory education for girls and boys at the primary and secondary levels and improve women's economic and political empowerment.

THE LEAGUE'S POSITION

The League of Women Voters supports a strong, effective United Nations and endorses the full and active participation of the United States in the UN system. The League supports UN efforts to:

- Promote international peace and security
- Advance the social and economic well-being of the world's people
- Ensure respect for human rights and fundamental freedoms
- Foster trust and cooperation among nations by encouraging adherence to conventions, treaties, and other international agreements
- Protect the integrity of the world environment
- Achieve the full and equal participation of women in all aspects of civil and political life.

The United Nations should be an important component of U.S. foreign policy. The League supports U.S. policies that strengthen the UN's capacity to solve global problems and promote prosperity throughout the world. The United States should work actively and constructively within the UN system, exercising diplomatic leadership in advance of decision-making. The United States should not place conditions on its participation in the UN, except in the most extreme cases, such as flagrant violations of the Charter.

The League supports UN leadership in a comprehensive, multi-faceted approach to promoting world peace and security that includes ongoing efforts to eliminate the underlying causes of conflict. UN peace operations should include such strategies as:

- An increased emphasis on preventive diplomacy and the use of such techniques as an early warning system to identify possible threats to peace and mediation to help resolve disputes
- Preventive deployment of UN peacekeepers to forestall the outbreak of hostilities
- Enhanced capacity to respond rapidly and effectively to contain conflict and establish a just and stable peace
- UN peacekeeping operations that have strong political and financial support from the world community and the consent of the local parties
- Military intervention, as a last resort, to halt genocide and other crimes against humanity and to prevent the spread of conflict
- Protection of civilian populations, including protection of displaced persons
- Long-term commitment, both pre- and post-conflict, to establishing the institutions and conditions needed for real economic and social development
- Enhanced capacity at UN headquarters to plan, manage and support UN peace operations.

The United States should support all aspects of UN peace operations. Non-governmental organizations (NGOs) have an important role to play in peace operations, including participating in behind-the-scenes diplomatic efforts and providing humanitarian aid.

The League strongly supports the central role of the United Nations in addressing the social, economic and humanitarian needs of all people. The advancement and empowerment of women is fundamental to achieving peace and prosperity and should be a high priority for UN programs. Other areas for emphasis include:

- Eradicating poverty and hunger
- Improving basic living standards worldwide
- Promoting the well-being and potential of children, with special attention to the girl child
- Promoting human and political rights

- Ensuring access to a basic education for all
- Ensuring a basic level of health care for all
- Protecting the environment and the world's natural resources.

The League supports efforts to strengthen the development and humanitarian work of the United Nations through greater coordination among agencies, more efficient use of resources, additional funding as required, and more partnerships with NGOs and other non-state actors. UN-sponsored world conferences are valuable forums for building international consensus and developing practical plans of action to solve global problems.

The United States should provide strong leadership and financial support to the UN specialized agencies, participate constructively in international conferences, and fulfill all agreed-upon commitments.

The League believes that world peace and progress rest in part on a body of international law developed through conventions, covenants, and treaties and on the judgments of international courts. Disputes between nations should be considered and settled in the International Court of Justice, and its judicial decisions should be honored.

The League supports the creation of a permanent international tribunal, such as the International Criminal Court, to try individuals charged with crimes of genocide, war crimes, and other systematic crimes against humanity.

All court procedures must meet the highest judicial standards, including guarantees of due process protections and the integrity and impartiality of the courts' officials.

The League supports full U.S. participation in the international judicial system and U.S. ratification and observance of international treaties and conventions consistent with LWVUS principles and positions.

The League supports the basic principles of the UN Charter. The League supports one-nation, one-vote in the General Assembly, the veto power in the Security Council, and a strong, effective office of the Secretary-General. **The League supports measures to make the Security Council a more representative body that better reflects the diverse interests of UN member nations and the world's people. The United States should work to encourage member nations to consider the needs of the world as a whole and avoid divisive politicization of issues.**

Member nations have the collective responsibility to provide the resources necessary for the UN to carry out its mandates, with each providing financial contributions commensurate with its ability to pay. The United States should meet its financial obligations to the UN on time, in full, and without conditions.

Statement of Position on the United Nations, as Announced by National Board, June 1977 and Updated, June 2002.

TRADE

The League's long-standing interest in world trade has its origins in a 1920 study of high postwar prices. This study and another on the economic causes of war convinced the League that high tariffs and restrictive trade practices add to consumer prices, reduce competition in the marketplace and cause friction among nations. The Depression accentuated the impact of high tariffs and moved the League to take action for the first time on trade matters. Since then, the League has been involved with every major piece of trade legislation, always strongly supporting measures that expand rather than restrict trade.

After an extensive reappraisal in the early 1960s, the League urged that the United States systematically reduce trade barriers, delegate long-term, flexible negotiating authority to the executive and use trade adjustment assistance as a positive alternative to import restrictions. In 1965, the League added another dimension: support for measures to

relax restrictions on trade with Eastern Europe and the Soviet Union. The 1972 Convention, during a time of dollar devaluation and balance-of-trade deficits, asked Leagues to reexamine trade policies to find new ways to help the economy adjust to changing trade patterns, especially measures to counter rising protectionist sentiment. The revised 1973 position in support of liberal trade policies placed a new emphasis on expanding and improving adjustment assistance programs.

The League vigorously supported the Trade Act of 1974, which led to U.S. participation in the Tokyo Round of tariff negotiations under the auspices of the General Agreement on Tariffs and Trade (GATT). In 1979, the League mounted a major lobbying effort to assure implementation of the Tokyo Round of multilateral trade negotiations (MTN) agreements designed to establish a fair, open and disciplined trading structure for the next decade. Throughout the five years of negotiations, the League worked to deflect protectionist efforts in Congress to block the negotiations. Through its efforts, the League helped assure overwhelming passage of the Trade Agreements Act of 1979, the largest single trade bill in U.S. history. Attempts to undermine the trade agreements have been vigorously opposed by the League.

The League also has been instrumental in promoting measures to improve trade opportunities for developing countries and in defeating protectionist amendments to foreign assistance appropriation bills. The League strongly supported the Trade and International Economic Policy Reform Act of 1987 and worked to defeat restrictive amendments.

In 2002, the League voiced its opposition to providing the President with new negotiating authority for trade agreements because the proposed authority did not adequately provide for protecting environmental, labor and political values as part of trade agreements.

THE LEAGUE'S POSITION
The League of Women Voters of the United States supports a liberal U.S. trade policy aimed at reducing trade

barriers and expanding international trade. Such a policy helps foster international cooperation, democratic values, and economic prosperity at home and abroad as well as benefiting consumers through lowered prices, expanded choice and improved products and services. The League believes that U.S. trade policy should be based on the long-term public interest, not on special interests, and should advance the achievement of other important policy goals, including:

- Improve of basic living standards worldwide
- Reduction of inequalities within and among nations
- Protection of the environment and global natural resources
- Respect for human, labor, religious and political rights
- Improve labor conditions around the world.

The League endorses the worldwide systematic reduction of tariffs, subsidies and quotas. The League also supports the reduction of non-tariff barriers to trade consistent with the goals and strategies set forth in this position statement. Administrative and customs procedures should be efficient and flexible.

The League supports U.S. participation in an international trade organization aimed at promoting worldwide economic growth via an open trading system. This organization should have the power to hold nations accountable for commitments made in multilateral trade treaties and should recognize the legitimacy of international agreements in the areas of the environment, labor, and human rights. Its proceedings should be open to scrutiny by the public, the press, and non-governmental organizations. The public should have timely access to a wide range of its documents, and its dispute settlement process should allow friend-of-the-court briefs.

The organization should recognize the legitimacy of a country's measures in the areas of the environment, health, labor and human rights that are more stringent than international standards or than those of its trading partners. These measures should not discriminate between domestic products and imports and should not be used as a pretext for restricting the flow of trade. The League believes that trade agreements should be negotiated multilaterally in the broadest possible international forum. Regional and bilateral trade agreements can be useful steppingstones to broader trade liberalization but should not be allowed to block progress in multilateral negotiations nor to marginalize poor countries.

The League believes the U.S. trade policy-making process should be open, transparent, and efficient and should advance League trade policy goals. The President should be given the authority to negotiate trade agreements within prior guidelines and conditions set by Congress. Congress should have an adequate but limited time period to debate and accept or reject the resulting proposed agreements, without amendment. Congress should take an active part in the policy-making process, establishing trade priorities and negotiating objectives and observing and monitoring trade negotiations. Congress should have the resources and staff expertise necessary to fulfill its trade responsibilities. The trade policy-making processes of both Congress and the executive branch should include meaningful opportunities for input from a broad range of public interest perspectives, as well as from business interests, and should include timely assessment of the impact of proposed trade agreements.

The League supports a variety of trade-related strategies to protect the environment and promote labor, political, religious and human rights, including

- Trade negotiations and trade agreements that lead to progress on environmental and social objectives
- Monitoring and reporting of countries' practices and performance in these areas
- Recognition of the legitimacy of multilateral environmental agreements
- Strengthening the International Labor Organization (ILO) and promoting ratification of ILO core labor rights

- Promoting ratification of the Universal Declaration of Human Rights and similar international agreements
- International sanctions aimed at ending egregious violations of human rights
- Legitimate labeling and certification programs (e.g., eco-labeling)
- Protection of endangered species
- Elimination of environmentally and economically harmful subsidies and incentives (e.g., for fishing, timber, agriculture)
- Codes of conduct to encourage responsible business practices in these areas (e.g., guarding against abusive child labor)
- Domestic regulations and practices that advance environmental and social goals and that are not a pretext for restricting trade
- Aid to developing countries to improve their ability to create and enforce national laws protecting the environment and human and labor rights.

The League supports trade and related policies that address the special needs of developing countries, with emphasis on economic growth and improving income distribution. The League supports such measures as:

- Priority elimination of tariffs and quotas on exports of developing countries
- Longer adjustment periods and financial and technical assistance for implementation of trade commitments
- Special measures to ensure access to essential medicines
- Financial and technical assistance to enable developing countries to participate effectively in the world trading system
- Financial aid for infrastructure improvements
- Policies that recognize the special circumstances of developing countries in the areas of food security and transition to the world trading system

The League supports strong U.S. leadership in, and financial support of, international institutions and programs that reduce poverty and address the special needs of developing countries in the areas of the environment and human and labor rights.

The League supports measures to address the adverse impact of international trade on domestic workers, firms and industries. Training, education and safety net programs, such as cash assistance, relocation assistance, and health care, should be enhanced and made easily available to dislocated workers, whether or not a trade connection can be made. Portability of health care coverage, pension rights and other fringe benefits should also be assured. The League supports temporary trade barriers consistent with international trade rules to permit firms seriously injured by surging import competition to adjust to changed conditions.

Statement of Position on Liberal Trade Policies, as Announced by National Board, June 1973 and Updated, April 2002.

U.S. RELATIONS WITH DEVELOPING COUNTRIES

The League's work on development issues began in the 1920s, when members studied the economic and social work of various international organizations. In 1940, the League studied proposals for closer economic and cultural relations between the United States and other American republics, including possible financial and technical cooperation. After World War II, the League supported the implementation of the Marshall Plan and President Truman's Point Four technical assistance program as part of its commitment to international efforts to support the poor and emerging nations of Asia, Africa, the Middle East and Latin America.

The League's position on Development Assistance evolved through two restudies in 1964 and 1970. The latter reiterated the need for separating development from military aid. The League supported the "basic needs" approach mandated by Congress in 1973 and adopted by the Agency for International Development (AID).

In the 1980s, the League's Development Assistance position was revised to reflect the results of the study of U.S. Relations with Developing Countries. Members reviewed current trends in trade, development assistance and the United Nations. They also examined U.S. commitments to developing countries, criteria for evaluating development and military assistance and the role of U.S.-Soviet relations in determining U.S. policies toward developing countries.

The resulting 1986 position emphasizes development assistance over military assistance as the most effective means of meeting the long-term social and economic needs of developing countries and downplays the role of international competition in determining U.S. policies toward developing countries. In 1986, the League urged Congress to reject aid that included military assistance to Nicaraguan counter-revolutionaries ("contras") and address the region's long-term social and economic needs. In 1987, the League pressured Congress to increase development and humanitarian aid in the foreign aid budget.

In the 1990s, the LWVEF began a series of global outreach projects which led to the current Global Democracy Program. "Thinking Globally" was designed to educate Americans about the links between their communities and the developing world.

Europe

Outreach in Europe in the 1990s led to the Global Community Dialogue program in 1992 with the Building Political Participation in Poland initiative and subsequent citizen exchange projects to share grassroots skills with citizens in Hungary, Russia, Ukraine, the American Republics and Africa.

In 1996, the LWVEF opened a U.S. coordination office for absentee voting in the post-war elections in Bosnia and Herzegovina. In an unprecedented effort to enfranchise Bosnian refugees and displaced persons residing in 55 countries for elections in 1996, 1997 and 1998, the League worked with the Organization for Security and Cooperation in Europe on the Bosnian Citizen Get-Out-the-Vote Campaign. The LWVEF formed a partnership with the League of Women Voters in Bosnia and Herzegovina to help women take an effective role in the post-war reconstruction process.

Since 2005, the League has participated in The Open World Leadership Center's Civic Hosting Program, first introducing Russian leaders to U.S. democracy and subsequently hosting visitors from Ukraine and Central Asia.

Africa

Outreach in Africa started in the late 1990s when the LWVEF joined Civitas Africa to share methodologies, tools and experiences with civic education groups. A citizen exchange program in Sub-Saharan Africa with grassroots organizations and activists, The Woman Power in Politics: Building Grassroots Democracy in Africa program was initiated with League members traveling to Africa as co-trainers in democracy-building skills until 2002. The League also worked with four nongovernmental organizations in Malawi to train thousands of poll monitors as civil society observers on Election Day 2004. It joined with the National Council of Women of Kenya to sponsor the Kenyans Working Together for Good Governance: Civil Society, Government and Members of Parliament program in 2006, including an exchange program between Kenyan citizens and League staff.

The Americas

Outreach in the Americas began with the Making Democracy Work in the Americas program at the Vital Voices of the Americas conference in 1998, followed by the League hosting women civic leaders and officials from Latin America in 1999.

In the 2000s, the League completed a successful program in Brazil called Women in Political Leadership, was invited by the International Foundation for Election Systems (IFES) to join a team of International Election Observers for Paraguayan elections, sponsored the program Women in the Americas: Paths to Political Power, and participated in a State Department sponsored exchange titled Connecting Civil Society and Future Legislators from Colombia and Brazil.

The League continued its efforts to work with women around the world in 2010-2012. During this period the League attended an international conference in La Havana, Cuba, organized by the Gender Department of the University of La Havana titled Women in the XXI Century. The League also accepted invitations to work with women in democratic transitions in Tunisia and Egypt in North Africa; in Antananarivo, Madagascar, in Africa; in Dhaka, Bangladesh in South Asia; and in Belgrade, Serbia in Southeast Europe.

In early 2012 citing the League's outstanding record of non-partisanship in advocating and promoting informed political participation in government, the U.S. Government selected the League to serve as its nongovernmental partner in the 2012 G8 Broader Middle East and North Africa (BMENA) Initiative.

The year-long initiative had as its ultimate goal to achieve agreement among the G8 and region foreign ministers on the language of the final declaration of the 9th Forum for the Future, the culminating meeting of the initiative. The second goal was to achieve civil society and private sector agreement on the recommendations forwarded to the governments. Both goals were achieved due to a steady building of trust among the participants as a result of the hard work of the League, the U.S. Government, the Republic of Tunisia, and the three nongovernmental organizations.

THE LEAGUE'S POSITION

The League of Woomen Voters believes that U.S. interests in developing countries should reflect the reality of global interdependence. Paramount among these interests are reducing the risk of military conflict, promoting the sound management of global resources, protecting human rights, stimulating economic growth and improving the quality of life in developing countries. U.S. policies toward developing countries should not be based on maintaining U.S. preeminence.

The LWVUS strongly believes that development assistance, which is designed to meet the long-term social and economic needs of developing countries, is the most effective means of promoting legitimate U.S. interests. Military assistance and the direct military involvement of U.S. forces are not appropriate means to further the League's stated paramount interests in developing countries.

Developing countries should not be the pawns or the playing fields for geopolitical competition. The relationship between the superpowers should not be an important factor in determining U.S. policies toward developing countries. The LWVUS supports efforts to reduce international competition in developing countries, including:

- Enhancing the role of the United Nations and other multilateral organizations
- Supporting regional approaches to conflict resolution.
- Encouraging cooperative efforts to promote the sound management of global resources and improve the quality of life
- Promoting measures to reduce tensions and increase communication, including scientific and cultural exchanges and other cooperative programs.

Statement of Position on U.S. Relations with Developing Countries, as Announced by National Board, April 1986.

The League of Women Voters believes that long-term requirements for world peace, humanitarian obligations and long-range national interests demand U.S. policies that help developing countries reach self-sustaining economic growth.

League members understand that the development process encompasses more than economic growth and urge that the focus be on the human concerns of development and on an improved quality of life for the people of developing countries. U.S. development assistance policies should enhance human dignity and fulfill basic human needs. The policies should be coordinated with other development efforts, and they should respect cultural differences. The League favors greater participation by the recipient nations in the planning and execution of development programs. The development effort should be one of a partnership between developed and developing countries. Development programs should be long-range, adequately financed, effectively coordinated and administered.

League members recognize that population pressures affect all other aspects of the development process. The League supports U.S. efforts to assist other nations in their population planning programs, in accordance with the culture and mores of each country. The League also emphasizes strongly the importance of programs for nutrition, health, employment and education.

The League advocates that the proportion of U.S. assistance given through multilateral channels should be substantially increased, with concurrent efforts being made to strengthen the multilateral agencies where necessary.

The League deems it essential that the trend of reduced aid be reversed and that U.S. contributions for development assistance be increased.

League members believe that aid alone is not enough to meet the needs of developing countries. Measures other than direct grants and loans must be utilized. The League advocates such measures as reduced tied aid, prevention and relief of debt burdens, and changed patterns of trade. The U.S. government must ensure that its trade, monetary, political and military policies do not subvert the goals of its development policies. The League also urges active participation in the development process by the private sector.

The League recognizes the gross disparity in trading positions between developed and developing countries. The exports of developing countries must be expanded if they are to broaden their economic base and improve their peoples' standard of living. Because of their need

for greater access to U.S. and other industrialized countries' markets, the League favors generalized, temporary preferential tariff treatment and certain commodity arrangements for developing countries. The principle of reciprocity in trade agreements, which the League supports, should be waived in order to make special trade concessions to developing countries.

Statement of Position on International Development Assistance, as Announced by National Board, April 1970 and Revised, April 1986.

The League of Women Voters believes that private investment of U.S. capital in developing countries can be an important supplemental means of helping these countries reach self-sustaining economic growth. In order to facilitate the flow of private capital to those developing countries that most need it and that can use it most advantageously, appropriate safeguards are necessary against risks for both the investor and the developing countries.

In order to protect outside investors against risks, the League favors continuation of governmental assistance, such as pre-investment surveys, investment guarantees and investment loans. The League believes that tax credits on funds invested in developing countries could provide additional encouragement.

In order to guard against risks for the developing country, the League believes that investors should be encouraged to engage in joint-venture type investments with local businesses, to seek matching investment funds within the country, to employ and train as high a proportion of local personnel as possible for responsible positions, and to send to these countries carefully chosen and well-briefed U.S. representatives. The League welcomes continued efforts by developing countries to encourage their citizens to invest more in their own countries' development efforts and to create a more favorable climate for public and private investment through appropriate internal reforms.

International commodity arrangements serve as a short-term supplement to long-run efforts to promote self-sustaining growth in developing countries.

Insofar as commodity arrangements can help moderate sharp fluctuations in the price of primary products and help stabilize the export income of developing countries, they can serve a useful, though necessarily short-term, purpose.

Each commodity arrangement should be evaluated on its own merit. Such arrangements should be flexible and open to renegotiation within a reasonable period of time.

Each arrangement needs careful supervision and regular review in order not to inhibit diversification within these countries of land, labor and capital or to distort international patterns of trade. These arrangements might include such compensatory financing efforts as those initiated under the International Monetary Fund.

If any commodity arrangement is to bear fruit, primary-product countries should be encouraged through technical and financial assistance to diversify both their primary-product and industrial position. If diversification efforts are not to be frustrated, the developed countries, including the U.S., need to open their export doors wider to a broader range of imports, whether raw materials, semi-processed or finished goods. In order to help the U.S. meet new competition, greater use might be made of trade adjustment assistance to affected U.S. industries and workers.

The League recognizes that continuation of freer trade policies and reduction of various trade barriers are essential to improve the terms of trade of developing countries.

Statement of Position on Private Investment and Commodity Arrangements, as Announced by National Board, April 1964 and Revised, April 1970.

ARMS CONTROL

The League's 1982-84 national security study was intended to add focus and direction to existing support for "efforts to reduce the risk of war, including negotiations on disarmament and arms control" under the UN position. Once the 1983 position was reached, League action in support of arms control measures was immediate and effective, particularly on the issues of the Strategic Defense Initiative (SDI)—a missile defense plan that undermines the 1972 Anti-Ballistic Missile (ABM) Treaty and anti-satellite weapons. The League has continued to play a key role in legislative efforts to limit funding for unworkable and destabilizing missile defense systems and to uphold the traditional interpretation of the ABM Treaty.

Other arms control measures supported by the League include: negotiation of a bilateral, mutually verifiable freeze on the testing, production and deployment of nuclear weapons to be followed by reductions; a comprehensive test ban treaty; and the Chemical Weapons Convention.

In 1988, the League was successful in lobbying for Senate ratification of the Intermediate Nuclear Forces Treaty (INF), an unprecedented agreement between the United States and the Soviet Union to eliminate an entire class of nuclear weapons. In October 1991, the League urged the Senate to ratify the Conventional Forces in Europe Treaty.

The League lobbied for ratification of the Comprehensive Test Ban Treaty (CTBT) from 1997 until October 1999 when Senate arms control opponents brought the treaty up without full hearings and the Senate rejected the resolution of ratification.

In 2000, the League again worked in support of the ABM Treaty and in opposition to deployment of a planned national missile defense (NMD) system.

After extensive review by a Board-appointed task force, the League's position was updated at Convention 2010 by concurrence of League delegates. In 2010, the LWVUS successfully lobbied for the new START Treaty between the

United States and Russia. In 2011, the Treaty, which includes new verification requirements for deployed strategic warheads as well as delivery vehicles, was ratified and signed.

THE LEAGUE'S POSITION

The League of Women Voters believes that arms control measures are essential to reduce the risk of war and increase global stability.

Toward that end, the U.S. government should give the highest level of importance to arms control efforts that:

- Limit or reduce the quantity of weapons
- Limit proliferation and prohibit first use of nuclear weapons
- Prohibit first use and possession of chemical, biological and radiological weapons
- Prohibit explosive testing of nuclear weapons
- Reduce tensions in order to prevent situations in which weapons might be used.

While these objectives should receive the highest level of attention, the U.S. government also should negotiate measures that inhibit the development and improvement of weapons, particularly nuclear weapons, that increase incentives to attack first in a period of crisis.

As a goal of international negotiations, the League supports the worldwide elimination of nuclear weapons.

The League of Women Voters recognizes that peace in an interdependent world is a product of cooperation among nations and therefore strongly favors multilateral negotiations. Leadership by the U.S. in advancing arms control measures through negotiations and periodic review is encouraged.

Given the potential for worldwide proliferation of nuclear technology, efforts involving all countries are essential to limit the spread of nuclear weapons and to protect commonly held nuclear weapons-free regions such as the seabed and outer space. Multilateral efforts are appropriate as well to achieve bans on the possession of chemical, biological and radiological weapons, and to achieve limitations on the transfer or trade of all weapons.

The League of Women Voters also supports bilateral arms control efforts, which may be especially appropriate in negotiations to limit, safeguard and reduce quantities of weapons. The League believes that unilateral initiatives are not the most appropriate means to achieve arms control.

The League does not support tying progress in arms control to other issues. The League believes that arms control is too important in and of itself and too crucial to all nations to be linked to other foreign and military policy goals.

The League of Women Voters believes that arms control measures should be evaluated in terms of the following factors:

EQUITY - The terms should be mutually beneficial, and each nation's security and interests should be adequately protected, as should the security of all nations. Equity does not necessarily require equality in numbers of weapons but may be achieved through a relative balance in capabilities.

VERIFIABILITY - Each party should be able to ensure that other parties comply with the terms of the agreement, whether using national technical means (such as satellites, seismic sensors and electronic monitors) or on-site inspection. The League recognizes the role that multilateral and international institutions can play in assisting verification efforts and believes it is extremely important to ensure compliance, acknowledging that absolute certainty is unattainable.

EQUITY AND VERIFIABILITY — Both are critical in efforts to limit and reduce quantities of weapons and to prohibit the possession and spread of nuclear weapons.

CONFIDENCE-BUILDING - Each party should be assured of the political or military intentions of other parties. Fostering confidence is vital in efforts to stem the development and proliferation of weapons and prohibit their first use and to reduce tensions.

WIDESPREAD AGREEMENT - All appropriate parties should participate in and approve the results of the negotiating process. However, the League recognizes that, in specific cases, progress can be achieved even though some key parties do not participate.

ENVIRONMENTAL PROTECTION - The quality of the earth's environment should be protected from the effects of weapons testing or use. Environmental protection has special significance in negotiations regarding all weapons of mass destruction as well as conventional weapons that have residual effects.

CONTINUITY - Negotiations should build on past agreements and should be directed toward future negotiations whenever feasible. Innovative thinking and new approaches should, however, be encouraged when appropriate.

Statement of Position on Arms Control, as Announced by National Board, December 1983 and Updated by the 2010 Convention.

FURTHER GUIDELINES
League's support of arms control measures includes actions on proposals, negotiations and agreements.

The League supports efforts to achieve quantitative limits or reductions that focus on nuclear warheads, non-nuclear weapons of mass destruction, missiles and other delivery systems, antiballistic missiles, conventional weapons or troop levels.

The League advocates limits on the spread or proliferation of weapons, nuclear technology, and fissile materials. The League opposes the proliferation of weapons, nuclear technology and fissile materials to non-state actors or to commonly held areas such as the seabed or outer space. The League supports establishing effective international monitoring, accounting and control of such transfers.

The League's pursuit of bans on the possession or use of weapons may apply to existing weapons or those not yet developed.

The League seeks to reduce tensions through better means of communication, exchange of information or prior notification of military tests and maneuvers in order to avoid the risks of miscalculation or accident. Other measures supported by the League to reduce tensions and create a climate of trust among nations include: scientific and cultural exchanges, conflict resolution training, and strengthening the UN and its supporting agencies. The League encourages efforts to mediate regional issues and arrive at negotiated settlements to minimize arms build-ups and avoid conflicts. The U.S. should keep lines of communication open.

The League supports efforts to inhibit the development and improvement of weapons through qualitative limits, including limits on testing of weapons. These constraints may be selective or comprehensive in their application.

Efforts to improve the arms control regime of international laws, oversight bodies and verification modalities are also supported, and U.S. engagement and leadership in this regard is encouraged. The League supports diligence by the U.S. in meeting the terms of ratified arms control agreements and in reviewing their effectiveness over time.

MILITARY POLICY AND DEFENSE SPENDING
The second part of the League's 1982-84 national security study focused on military policy objectives and defense spending, including spending priorities and links between defense and domestic spending in the federal budget. League members first evaluated U.S. military missions, then scrutinized military forces and defense budget priorities. This comprehensive approach stemmed from the principle that weapons systems should reflect a nation's military policy, which in turn should be developed from basic military purposes or missions. The resulting April 1984 statement related military policy and defense spending.

League action focused on congressional efforts to limit deployment of the MX missile and to oppose funding for a railroad based system. The League also has strongly opposed funding for the Strategic Defense Initiative (SDI) since 1985 and has been part of successful efforts to limit spending increases for the SDI program. Since the mid-1980s the League has called on Congress and the President to focus on defense spending when making budget cuts for deficit reduction.

As a result of the 1984-1986 study of U.S. Relations with Developing Countries, the Military Policy and Defense Spending position was revised to emphasize that "Military assistance and the direct military involvement of U.S. forces are not appropriate means to further the League's stated paramount interests in developing countries."

THE LEAGUE'S POSITION

The League of Women Voters believes the U.S. government should seek to protect its interests at home and abroad through the use of nonmilitary measures, including diplomacy, mediation and multilateral cooperation. These measures reflect the importance that the League attaches to U.S. efforts to strengthen international organizations, reduce tensions among nations and minimize the risk of conflict worldwide.

The League believes that military force should be viewed as a tool of last resort. Unquestionably, defense of the homeland is an appropriate military objective. In this context, conventional weapons are clearly preferable to nuclear weapons. Any decision to defend another nation militarily should be in support of clear foreign policy goals and tailored to specific circumstances. Military assistance and the direct military involvement of U.S. forces are not appropriate means to further the League's stated paramount interests in developing countries.

The League believes that nuclear weapons should serve only a limited and specific function, that of deterring nuclear attack on the U.S., until such time as these weapons are eliminated through arms-control and disarmament agreements. The goal of U.S. military policy,

however, should be to ensure that nuclear weapons are never used.

NUCLEAR DETERRENCE

The League believes that the United States should vigorously pursue arms-control negotiations in order to ensure that all nations reduce and eventually eliminate their stockpiles of strategic nuclear weapons. The League does not support unilateral elimination of any leg of the strategic nuclear triad of intercontinental ballistic missiles (ICBMs), submarine-launched ballistic missiles (SLBMs) and long-range bombers. However, the League does not support any modernization of the land leg that would result in weapons systems that are vulnerable or increase incentives to attack first.

NORTH ATLANTIC TREATY ORGANIZATION (NATO)

The League believes that the defense of NATO allies should continue to be a shared responsibility. The League supports the commitment of the U.S. to defend NATO allies with conventional forces. The League urges continued efforts to negotiate mutual and balanced reductions in conventional forces in Europe.

The League believes there is no appropriate role for U.S. nuclear weapons in the defense of NATO allies. The League strongly opposes the policy of threatening to introduce nuclear weapons into a conventional conflict in Europe, a policy commonly referred to as "first use." Consistent with these views, the League opposes the deployment of U.S. nuclear weapons on European soil.

OTHER COMMITMENTS

The League supports the U.S. commitment to defend Japan with conventional forces. Conventional forces also are appropriate for defending other allies. The League rejects any nuclear role in defending Japan and other allies, in protecting access to vital resources or in responding to military conflicts around the world.

DEFENSE SPENDING

The League believes that defense spending should be examined in the same way as spending for other national needs. Within any given level of defense funding, the U.S. should move toward emphasizing readiness over investment. Preference should be given to operations and maintenance expenditures and military pay as opposed to research and development, procurement of new weapons and construction of military facilities. The League believes that savings in the defense budget can be achieved through increased efficiency and improved accountability.

In summary, the League believes that national security has many dimensions and cannot be limited to military policy alone. It can be defined as ensuring domestic tranquility, providing for the common defense and promoting the general welfare. Key elements include the country's ability to implement social and environmental programs and to maintain cooperative relationships with other nations. Other important components are effective political leadership and a strong economy. Therefore, in decisions about the federal budget, political leaders should assess the impact of U.S. military spending on the nation's economy and on the government's ability to meet social and environmental needs.

Statement of Position on Military Policy and Defense Spending, as Announced by National Board, April 1984 and Revised, April 1986.

NATURAL RESOURCES

Promote an environment beneficial to life through the protection and wise management of natural resources in the public interest.

League members became concerned about depletion and conservation of natural resources as far back as the 1920s and 1930s when the League undertook a study of flood control, erosion and the creation of the Tennessee Valley Authority. Water resources were the focus of activities in the 1950s, and with the nascent environmental movement in the 1970s, the League built a broad national program focused on protecting and managing the interrelated aspects of air, water, land use, energy and waste management. Since then, the League has been in the forefront of the environmental protection movement, helping to frame landmark legislation and seeking to preserve and protect life-supporting ecosystems and public health. Fighting to improve opportunities for public participation on natural resource issues has always been a League theme, in addition to the substantive concerns that the League has pushed.

The League's citizen activists helped pass the landmark Clean Water Act in the early 1970s and worked to protect, expand and strengthen it through the 1990s. Water issues, from groundwater protection to agricultural runoff to the Safe Drinking Water Act, have energized League leaders, especially at the local level, for decades. Solid and hazardous waste issues and recycling also have been the focus of strong state and local action, and the federal legislative fights for the Resource Conservation and Recovery Act and Superfund focused on those issues as well.

The League has been a leader in fighting back efforts to gut the Clean Air Act from the early 1980s to the present. It pushed for acid rain and toxics controls as the act was reauthorized in 1990, building on the successful work of the previous decade in controlling the worst air pollution from automobiles and industrial sources. In the 2000s, the League not only fought to protect the Clean Air Act, but also turned attention to combatting global climate change.

With its work on energy policy beginning in the late 1970s, the League began a decades-long push for energy conservation and the use of renewable resources. As global climate change emerged as a key environmental and international issue in the late 1990s, energy conservation, renewable resources and air pollution controls took on new significance and the League's interrelated approach to natural resource issues proved farsighted. Understanding the need for global solutions to many environmental problems, the LWVUS has urged full U.S. participation in international efforts.

In the late 2000s, the League lobbied vigorously for comprehensive legislation to control global climate change by setting a cap on greenhouse gas pollution and by encouraging conservation and renewable energy. As part of an education and advocacy project on climate change, six state Leagues held forums with trips by the League President to speak at public events and meet with key Senators and staff. In early 2010, the LWVUS president was honored with a "Sisters on the Planet Climate Leader Award" by Oxfam America for the League's grassroots work on climate change.

In 2011 the League launched the Clean Air Promise Campaign. The campaign was developed to raise awareness of the dangers of harmful pollutants like industrial carbon, mercury and other air toxicants that created a growing threat to the health of our children and seniors. Seven state Leagues engaged in the project and raised awareness in their local communities, at the state and local levels of their governments while generating media attention about the growing problem of climate change caused by industrial carbon pollution. The LWVUS released television ads in Massachusetts and Missouri that called attention to votes taken by Senators Brown and McCaskill that would have blocked new air pollution standards for carbon. By demonstrating the political saliency of the climate change issue and the effects on human health, the ads succeeded in discouraging the Senate from taking up legislation that would undermine efforts to address climate change.

The League continues its strong advocacy on climate issues by supporting the Presidents Climate Action Plan. The cornerstone of the plan, controls carbon pollution from new and existing power plants, which are the largest source of industrial carbon pollution in the U.S. In addition, the

League voiced support for "putting a price on carbon" to compliment the regulatory effort.

In the 2014–2016 biennium, the League continued work to fight climate change by supporting regulations from the Environmental Protection Agency, fighting legislation to stop or hurt progress on climate initiatives and by pushing for the full rejection of the Keystone XL pipeline. The League continued support for the EPA's Clean Power Plan and New Source Pollution Standard by participating in field hearings across the country and collecting comments from grassroots supporters in support of the regulations, all while working to fight legislation to overturn or weaken the regulations in Congress. The League strongly supported the People's Climate March in New York City and the UN Paris Agreement, which was an historic international agreement that established a commitment to reduce carbon pollution and fight climate change. Finally, the League endorsed regulations from EPA to reduce the levels of ozone in the atmosphere and regulate methane in the oil and gas sector.

In 1988, the LWVUS adopted a position on the role of the federal government in U.S. agriculture policy, which local and state Leagues also have applied to key action in their jurisdictions. A second position on Federal Agriculture Policies was adopted in 2014.

THE LEAGUE'S POSITION

The League of Women Voters believes natural resources should be managed as interrelated parts of life-supporting ecosystems. Resources should be conserved and protected to assure their future availability. Pollution of these resources should be controlled in order to preserve the physical, chemical and biological integrity of ecosystems and to protect public health.

Statement of Position on Natural Resources, as Affirmed by the 1986 Convention, Based on Positions Reached from 1958 Through 1986.

RESOURCE MANAGEMENT

The League's 1956-1958 water resources study was the basis for action on a broad range of resource management issues. By 1958, the League had taken a position that, as rephrased and expanded in 1960, has formed one of two foundations for League action on water ever since. The key concept is a strong federal role in formulating national policies and procedures.

The issue of water management led the League toward later interrelated positions on air pollution, solid waste disposal and land use, all focused on management policies to protect natural resources.

In 1970, the League recognized the need for federal control of air pollution and adopted a position for control of air emissions. The 1970 Convention also authorized a study of solid waste disposal, which focused League attention on re-use and recycling.

In 1972, Convention delegates voted to "evaluate land-use policies and procedures and their relationship to human needs, population trends and ecological and socioeconomic factors." The three-year land-use study focused on achieving optimum balance between human needs and environmental quality. Members agreed in 1975 that land ownership implies responsibilities of stewardship and consideration of public and private rights. They concluded that every level of government should share responsibility for land planning and management, and that federal policies should enhance the capabilities of other levels.

Although efforts in 1975 to pass comprehensive land-use legislation failed, the League has successfully supported more specialized land-use laws, notably coastal-zone planning and strip-mining controls.

Since 1982 most action on land use issues has been at the state and local levels. Many Leagues work on such issues as floodplain management, coastal-zone management, wetlands protection, open-space preservation, facility siting, transportation, wilderness designations and offshore energy development.

In the 1980s, the LWVUS lobbied for reauthorization and strengthening of the Coastal Zone Management (CZM) program, which provides federal funds for planning at the state level. The League also supports the Coastal Barrier Resources System, legislation that would eliminate federal flood insurance subsidies to barrier islands and other coastal areas subject to frequent storm action.

In 1990, the League provided testimony on Federal Reclamation Policy in support of legislation to eliminate abuses and close loopholes in the Reclamation Reform Act of 1982. Specifically, the League supported action to ensure compliance with the acreage limitations of the act and to reduce water subsidies that are uneconomical and environmentally destructive. In 1992, the League supported broad reform of the National Flood Insurance Program to increase enrollment and encourage risk management practices to reduce future losses.

League work on energy began in the early 1970s. In 1975, the LWVUS adopted a position supporting energy conservation as national policy. In 1976, the LWVUS Board approved guidelines to implement the position. Since then, the League has made conservation the crux of its energy agenda, recognizing that the conservation of energy guarantees major long-term environmental, economic and strategic benefits to individuals, the country and the world.

The 1976 Convention authorized a study to "evaluate sources of energy and the government's role in meeting future needs," which resulted in a broad 1978 position on energy policies and sources (including conservation) that is the basis for action on a wide variety of energy issues at all government levels. The 1979 Council recommended that the LWVUS Board review application of the Energy position to nuclear energy. The Board subsequently determined that the League would work to minimize reliance on nuclear fission.

The League advocates a national energy policy emphasizing increased fuel-efficiency standards for automobiles, opposition to oil drilling in environmentally sensitive areas including the Arctic National Wildlife Refuge (ANWR) and support for government action in the development and use of energy conservation and renewable energy sources.

Worldwide recognition of the global nature of environmental problems and the need for sustainable development came to the fore with the United Nations Conference on Environment and Development (UNCED) in Rio de Janeiro, Brazil in 1992. Leagues across the country hosted meetings to funnel citizen input into the UNCED agenda, and the LWVUS urged support for the Earth Summit's recommendations on global cooperation.

The League opposed efforts in the 104th Congress to pass "takings" legislation that would seriously undermine environmental protections in the name of "private property rights." While an extreme takings bill passed the House early in 1995, there was no Senate action. The League supported stewardship of critical resources, opposing congressional measures to transfer coastal lands from public to private hands.

In 2005, the League urged Congress to oppose energy legislation that would have wrongfully used the devastation of Hurricane Katrina and other disasters as a pretext for undermining important environmental protections.

Throughout the 2000s, the League continued its opposition to repeated efforts to drill for oil in the Arctic National Wildlife Refuge (ANWR). In 2006, the League submitted comments to the National Environmental Policy Act (NEPA) task force, urging its members to uphold the integrity of the original landmark legislation.

Early in 2012, the League declared its opposition to the proposed Keystone XL (KXL) Pipeline because of the need to put the U.S. on a path of emissions reductions, to protect against climate change and to ensure safe drinking water for all Americans. Later that year, the League commended the President's decision to delay the approval of the pipeline until appropriate study and consideration could be taken. The League also worked to encourage the President to veto legislation from Congress in 2015 that would have forced the approval of the KXL pipeline. The League continues to encourage a full rejection of the pipeline by the Executive Branch.

The League continues to lobby against legislation that would undermine clean air standards, make global climate change worse and fail to provide for needed energy conservation measures.

THE LEAGUE'S POSITION

The League of Women Voters believes resource management decisions must be based on a thorough assessment of population growth and of current and future needs. The inherent characteristics and carrying capacities of each area's natural resources must be considered in the planning process. Policy makers must take into account the ramifications of their decisions on the nation as a whole as well as on other nations.

To assure the future availability of essential resources, government policies must promote stewardship of natural resources. Policies that promote resource conservation are a fundamental part of such stewardship. Resources such as water and soil should be protected. Consumption of nonrenewable resources should be minimized. Beneficiaries should pay the costs for water, land and energy development projects. Reclamation and reuse of natural resources should be encouraged.

The League believes that protection and management of natural resources are responsibilities shared by all levels of government. The federal government should provide leadership, guidance and financial assistance to encourage regional planning and decision making to enhance local and state capabilities for resource management.

The League supports comprehensive long-range planning and believes that wise decision-making requires:

- Adequate data and a framework within which alternatives may be weighed and intelligent decisions made
- Consideration of environmental, public-health, social and economic impacts of proposed plans and actions
- Protection of private property rights commensurate with overall consideration of public health and environmental protection

- Coordination of the federal government's responsibilities and activities
- Resolution of inconsistencies and conflicts in basic policy among governmental agencies at all levels
- Regional, interregional and/or international cooperation when appropriate
- Mechanisms appropriate to each region that will provide coordinated planning and administration among units of government, governmental agencies and the private sector
- Procedures for resolving disputes
- Procedures for mitigation of adverse impacts
- Special responsibility by each level of government for those lands and resources entrusted to them
- Special consideration for the protection of areas of critical environmental concern, natural hazards, historical importance and aesthetic value
- Special attention to maintaining and improving the environmental quality of urban communities.

ENVIRONMENTAL PROTECTION AND POLLUTION CONTROL

Since the 1960s, the League has been at the forefront of efforts to protect air, land and water resources. Since the enactment of the Clean Air Act, the Clean Water Act, the Safe Drinking Water Act and the Resource Conservation and Recovery Act (RCRA), the League has worked for effective regulatory programs.

The League's pioneering focus on the interrelationships among air and water management issues forms the basis of efforts to ensure that government decision-making recognizes that environmental protection must be a seamless web. The evolution continues as the League's efforts go beyond fighting for pollution control and waste management strategies to demanding pollution prevention and waste reduction.

During the 1980s, the League fought hard to thwart attempts to weaken environmental protections through legislative and regulatory channels and severe federal budget cuts. League members pushed for strong environmental safeguards in the reauthorization of the Clean Air Act and the Clean Water Act. A League-endorsed reauthorization of the Superfund program proved a major step toward continuing the clean-up of the nation's hazardous waste sites. The 1990s and 2000s brought continued pressure to weaken environmental legislation and underfund programs. The League has continued to push for strong laws and full program funding for the U.S. Environmental Protection Agency, as well as for the defeat of across-the-board "regulatory reform" proposals that would weaken environmental protections.

Air Quality

After beginning its study of air pollution in 1970, the League reached its 1971 position in support of federal air pollution controls on industrial production, government installations, fuels and vehicles. The position opened the way for League action at the federal, state, regional and local levels.

Ever since, the League has pressed for full implementation of the Clean Air Act of 1970 and for strengthening amendments, while fighting against attempts to weaken it. Early on, the League opposed the continued extension of deadlines for meeting ambient air quality standards and auto-emission standards and supported visibility protection for national parks and the prevention of significant deterioration in program to protect air in relatively clean-air areas.

In the 1980s, the Clean Air Act came under strong attack, and the League helped lead the effort to protect and strengthen it. Finally, in 1990, League environmentalists were rewarded with passage of the 1990 Clean Air Act, which included major improvements to combat acid rain and smog and to cut emissions of toxicants. The legislation mandated major reductions in sulfur and nitrogen oxide emissions through the use of best available technology and energy efficiency. It attacked both stationary and mobile sources of pollutants. The Act set national standards and helped cities and states deal with local problems. The League at all levels worked to ensure full implementation of the revised Act.

The League has also worked for tighter fuel efficiency standards (Corporate Average Fuel Economy or CAFE standards) for automobiles to improve energy efficiency and reduce pollution.

In the 1990s, antiregulatory legislation gave Congress unprecedented authority to reject new regulations issued by federal agencies by passing a "resolution of disapproval." League members strenuously urged their members of Congress to oppose efforts to reject strengthened standards and the LWVUS strongly supported the EPA's issuance of new National Ambient Air Quality Standards (NAAQS) for ground-level ozone and fine particulate matter to protect public health. The League worked successfully to defeat amendments to the Intermodal Surface Transportation Efficiency Act (ISTEA) that would have allowed designated air quality funds to be spent on highway programs.

Following December 1997 treaty negotiations in Kyoto, Japan, on the Framework Convention on Climate Change, the League applauded the President's initiative to make the United States a world leader in combating global climate change and to seek negotiated, fair reductions and meaningful participation by developing countries in reducing greenhouse gases. League members lobbied against Senate passage of a resolution to oppose the "Kyoto Protocol," which called for nations to reduce their greenhouse gases, and they lobbied their senators to reject any actions that undermine international negotiations to stop climate change.

EPA instituted major new initiatives to clean up the air during 1998-2000, and the League worked to see them promulgated. The League commented on EPA's proposed new emissions standards for SUVs (sport utility vehicles) and heavy vehicles, arguing for the importance of controlling the mobile sources of air pollution that had largely gone unregulated.

In 1999-2000, while Congress fought to a standstill over clean air issues, the League produced a Q&A on Global Warming, a valuable resource for citizens on this key issue. The LWVUS believes that climate change is a serious problem that requires immediate international action. The League believes the U.S. government should move ahead immediately, without waiting for other nations, on initiatives to reduce emissions of heat-trapping gases. Such actions will reduce the threat of global climate change, combat air pollution, increase energy security and create new jobs.

In the 2000s, energy legislation became the primary vehicle for attempts to weaken the Clean Air Act. The League worked throughout the 2000s to block these efforts. In the later 2000s, the LWVUS significantly increased its advocacy concerning global climate change legislation. In 2006, the League and other concerned organizations submitted a statement to the U.S. Environmental Protection Agency urging strengthened air quality standards consistent with the Clean Air Act. Later that year, the League joined other groups in issuing a statement of principles on the importance of reducing climate change. The League also created a Climate Change Task force.

In 2008, the League called on Congress to enact legislation to significantly cut the greenhouse gas emissions which cause global climate change and supported increased energy efficiency and a shift to a clean, renewable energy. The League called for a moratorium on the building of new coal-fired electric power plants and supported requirements for utilities to produce a significant percentage of electricity from renewable resources.

The League supported the Climate Security Act of 2008, as well as amendments to strengthen the bill. This legislation provided for a cap and trade system, which would have cut greenhouse gas emission from electric power generation, transportation and manufacturing sources. The emissions cap would be reduced over time to meet pollution reduction goals based on the best-available scientific information. These emissions reductions could be traded on a market, set up by the legislation, allowing polluters to buy, sell, borrow and trade emission allowances to ensure economic efficiency in the program. The League also urged elected officials to extend clean energy tax incentives. Though it passed the House, the legislation was side-tracked in the Senate by special interests.

In December 2009, the League was thrilled to participate on the international stage, sending an official non-governmental organization delegation to Copenhagen, Denmark, for the UN Framework Convention on Climate Change. In March 2010, 19 League leaders from as many states were brought to Washington to lobby congressional leaders on strong climate change legislation. In addition, the Climate Change Task Force developed and promoted a "Toolkit for Climate Action" to assist Leagues and League members throughout the country in the fight to combat global climate change.

In 2012, when the EPA proposed the first-ever standards to control industrial carbon pollution from power plants, which causes global climate change and increases health problems, the League joined with its environmental and social justice allies in collecting the largest number of comments ever submitted in review of an EPA regulation. More than three million comments were submitted in support of the proposed rules for new power plants and urging EPA to take the next step and set carbon standards for existing plants.

With Congress unable or unwilling to act on climate change, in 2012, the League launched an initiative to urge the President to use his executive authority under the Clean Air Act to control carbon pollution from both new and existing power plants, which are the largest source of industrial carbon pollution in the U.S. The League strongly urged the President to lead the world in the right direction in the face of the greatest environmental challenge of our generation: climate change. With the proposed rules on new power plants in limbo and standards for new plants not yet proposed, the League used paid advertising, action alerts and new media tools to urge the President to get the job done.

Water Resources

Passage of an expanded Safe Drinking Water Act in 1986 and the Clean Water Act of 1987 marked important milestones in the League's effort to ensure safe drinking water for all Americans and safeguards against nonpoint pollution.

Groundwater, virtually unprotected by national legislation, became the focus of state and local League efforts in 1990, when the LWVEF undertook a project to increase citizen awareness of the importance of protecting groundwater supplies, the source of 50 percent of the nation's drinking water. Leagues in 17 states sponsored public forums, conferences, action guides and educational videos, "water-watcher" teams and media outreach. The local efforts were documented in a citizen handbook: *Protect Your Groundwater: Educating for Action*. In 1994, the LWVEF sponsored a national videoconference on groundwater protection with more than 140 downlink sites nationwide. The education efforts were complemented with LWVUS lobbying to address groundwater concerns in the renewal of the Clean Water Act of 1994.

Leagues across the country conducted surveys of local drinking water officials and held educational forums under the LWVEF Safe Drinking Water Project.

The project's publications, *Safety on Tap* and *Crosscurrents*, were used widely by Leagues and other citizen groups. In 1994 and 1995, the League opposed amendments to the Safe Drinking Water Act that would require EPA to conduct formal cost-benefit analyses with comparative risk analyses for every regulatory action and urged Congress to restore funding and adopt improvements to the act.

In 1997, the LWVEF sponsored a second, award-winning videoconference, "Tools for Drinking Water Protection," featuring protection strategies and mechanisms at work in diverse communities around the United States. It was downlinked to more than 750 sites in the United States, Puerto Rico, the Virgin Islands, Canada and Brazil, and allowed citizens, officials, business leaders and nongovernmental organizations to share information. It won the 1997 award for "Most Outstanding Broadcast for the Public Good" from the teleconferencing industry. In 1998, the LWVEF published *Strategies for Effective Public Involvement in Drinking Water Source Assessment and Protection*, a handbook to facilitate the public involvement required by the Safe Drinking Water Act Amendments of 1996.

The League also focused education efforts on wetlands protection. In 1996, the LWVEF held a Wetlands Protection Workshop, bringing together members from 23 states, national environmental specialists and local leaders to explore the value of coastal and freshwater wetlands, highlight measures and programs geared toward wetlands protection and examine methods for effective communication of wetlands information in local communities. In 1997-1998, the LWVEF provided pass-through grants to 11 Leagues to educate their communities on wetlands.

In 1998, the LWVUS supported the President's proposed action plan to crack down on polluted runoff and to restore and protect wetlands. In a related action, the League submitted comments to the Army Corps of Engineers urging revocation of Nationwide Permit 26 (NWP 26), which sanctions the loss of thousands of acres of wetlands every year.

In May 2000, the LWVEF sponsored "The Ech₂O Workshop: An Introduction to the Watershed Approach," where League activists learned how to take leadership in protecting their local watersheds and educating the public about watershed protection.

In February 2003, the LWVUS submitted comments to the EPA on attempts to redefine and limit the jurisdictional focus of the Clean Water Act, noting that the Clean Water Act covers all waters. "Whether large or small, they function as an interconnected system; excision of parts of the system [from regulation] will impair health and optimal functioning of the whole." The threat to streams and rivers from mountaintop removal, a coal-mining technique that can bury those water bodies was fought by the League.

In 2005, the League urged Senators to protect women and children from toxic mercury by supporting a bipartisan resolution to reject the Environmental Protection Agency's (EPA) rule to delay reductions in mercury emissions from power plants.

Delegates at the 2010 Convention shared information about hydraulic fracturing, commonly referred to as "fracking," a process by which high pressure water, sand and chemicals are pumped underground to fracture geologic formations in order to release natural gas. This process, as well as other fossil fuel extraction processes, poses a threat to water and other natural resources. State Leagues, using LWVUS positions on natural resources, particularly clean water and drinking water, worked to reduce the environmental impact of mining processes that contaminate and pollute.

In 2012, the LWVUS made its voice heard to several regulatory authorities of the federal government in relation to "fracking." Comments went to the Environmental Protection Agency (EPA), the Bureau of Land Management (BLM) and the Federal Energy Regulatory Commission (FERC). In 2015, the League supported a set of five bills referred to as the "Frack Pack." The legislation would help protect the environment and public health from the risks of hydraulic fracturing by ending exemptions for oil and gas production from major environmental laws such as the Safe Drinking Water Act.

Solid Waste

Work on solid waste began in 1971, when Leagues studied solid waste disposal in their home communities and then turned their attention to national policies on reuse, reclamation and recycling. By April 1973, members had reached agreement that solid waste should be regarded as a resource and that although the major responsibility should be at the state and local levels, the federal government should play a greater role in managing solid waste. Diminishing landfill capacity and a growing awareness of the pollution hazards of incineration brought concerns about interstate commerce in waste and renewed enthusiasm for recycling in the late 1980s. Leagues continue to support national and state recycling efforts, waste reduction measures and household hazardous waste collection programs.

By the late 1970s, League attention to hazardous waste resulted in two major victories at the federal level. The Resource Conservation and Recovery Act of 1976 (RCRA) provided for hazardous waste management programs, grants to states and localities for solid waste planning and implementation programs, and the Toxic Substance Control Act of 1976 (TSCA) regulated products that pose an unreasonable risk to human health or the environment.

During the 1980s the League continued to support reauthorization of these laws.

The League closely monitored RCRA implementation, commenting on proposed regulations and working for effective state programs. The League was a leader in efforts to pass legislation prohibiting the injection of toxic wastes into and above underground sources of drinking water, set location standards for siting waste-treatment, storage and disposal facilities, and permit land disposal of untreated hazardous waste only as a last resort for selected substances.

In the 1991-1994 battle over reauthorization of RCRA, the League strongly supported the "reduce, reuse, recycle" hierarchy. The League pushed for mandatory recycling measures including minimum recycled-content standards, a national bottle bill and a pause in the construction of municipal incinerators. The League urged the Administration to issue executive orders to promote recycling.

In 1992, the LWVEF published *Recycling Is More Than Collections,* a grassroots investigation of recycling conducted by League volunteers across the country. The LWVEF continued its educational work with publication of *The Garbage Primer* and *The Plastic Waste Primer* in 1993 and with citizen training programs.

The League also supported pollution prevention and community access to information on emissions, as well as measures to enable state and EPA regulators to compel federal facilities to comply with RCRA standards.

In 1980 the League helped pass the Comprehensive Environmental Response, Compensation and Liability Act (CERCLA), known as Superfund. The act authorized $1.6 billion over five years for the clean-up of the nation's toxic waste sites. Over the years, the League repeatedly has gone to Congress to ensure that a reauthorized Superfund contains adequate funding and safeguards to continue the job.

Nuclear Waste

The League pushed for congressional passage of the Low-Level Waste Policy Act in 1980 and the Nuclear Waste Policy Act in 1982 to ensure a national policy that incorporates adequate environmental safeguards with a strong role for public participation in nuclear-waste repository siting decisions. Leagues across the country have used League positions to support their involvement in the siting of low-level nuclear waste sites, high-level waste sites and nuclear power plants. The LWVEF has published a wide range of materials, including the acclaimed *Nuclear Waste Primer*. Following passage of the Nuclear Waste Policy Act of 1985, the LWVEF sponsored a public policy training program and published *The Nuclear Waste Digest*.

In 1992, the LWVEF signed a five-year cooperative agreement with the Department of Energy (DOE) to publish a third edition of *The Nuclear Waste Primer* (1993) and to conduct citizen education programs on nuclear waste. In 1995, the LWVEF launched a second five-year cooperative agreement with DOE to focus educational and citizen involvement efforts on defense waste management issues. In June 1998, the LWVEF held two regional intersite discussions on nuclear material and waste and issued a report to DOE.

In 1995, the LWVUS opposed congressional efforts to designate Yucca Mountain, NV, as a permanent or temporary repository for nuclear waste prior to studies verifying suitability. The League urged Congress to oppose the Nuclear Waste Policy Act of 1997, which mandated an interim storage site at Yucca Mountain. In 2002, the LWVUS lobbied in opposition making Yucca Mountain a permanent repository site for nuclear waste.

THE LEAGUE'S POSITION

The League of Women Voters supports the preservation of the physical, chemical and biological integrity of the ecosystem and maximum protection of public health and the environment. The League's approach to environmental protection and pollution control is one of problem solving. The interrelationships of air, water and land resources should be recognized in designing environmental safeguards. The League's environmental protection and anti-pollution goals aim to prevent ecological degradation and to reduce and control pollutants before they go down the sewer, up the chimney or into the landfill.

The League believes that although environmental protection and pollution control are responsibilities shared by all levels of government, it is essential that the federal government provide leadership and technical and financial assistance.

The federal government should have the major role in setting standards for environmental protection and pollution control. Other levels of government should have the right to set more stringent standards. Enforcement should be carried out at the lower levels of government, but the federal government should enforce standards if other levels of government do not meet this responsibility. Standards must be enforced in a timely, consistent and equitable manner for all violators in all parts of society, including governmental units, industry, business and individuals.

Environmental protection and pollution control, including waste management, should be considered a cost of providing a product or service. Consumers, taxpayers and ratepayers must expect to pay some of the costs. The League supports policies that accelerate pollution control, including federal financial assistance for state and local programs.

The League of Women Voters supports:

- Regulation of pollution sources by control and penalties
- Inspection and monitoring
- Full disclosure of pollution data
- Incentives to accelerate pollution control
- Vigorous enforcement mechanisms, including sanctions for states and localities that do not comply with federal standards and substantial fines for noncompliance.

FURTHER GUIDELINES AND CRITERIA

AIR QUALITY

The League of Women Voters supports:

- Measures to reduce vehicular pollution, including inspection and maintenance of emission controls, changes in engine design and fuel types and development of more energy- efficient transportation systems
- Regulation and reduction of pollution from stationary sources
- Regulation and reduction of ambient toxic-air pollutants
- Measures to reduce transboundary air pollutants, such as ozone and those that cause acid deposition.

ENERGY

The League of Women Voters supports:

- Energy goals and policies that acknowledge the United States as a responsible member of the world community
- Reduction of energy growth rates
- Use of a variety of energy sources, with emphasis on conserving energy and using energy-efficient technologies
- The environmentally sound use of energy resources, with consideration of the entire cycle of energy production
- Predominant reliance on renewable resources
- Policies that limit reliance on nuclear fission
- Action by appropriate levels of government to encourage the use of renewable resources and energy conservation through funding for research and development, financial incentives, rate-setting policies and mandatory standards
- Mandatory energy conservation measures, including thermal standards for building efficiency, new appliance standards and standards for new automobiles with no relaxation of auto-emission control requirements
- Policies to reduce energy demand and minimize the need for new generating capacity through techniques such as marginal cost or peak-load pricing or demand-management programs

- Maintaining deregulation of oil and natural gas prices
- Assistance for low-income individuals when energy policies bear unduly on the poor.

LAND USE

The League of Women Voters supports:

- Management of land as a finite resource not as a commodity, since land ownership, whether public or private, carries responsibility for stewardship
- Land-use planning that reflects conservation and wise management of resources
- Identification and regulation of areas of critical concern
- Fragile or historical lands, where development could result in irreversible damage (e.g., shore-lands of rivers, lakes and streams, estuaries and bays; rare or valuable ecosystems and geological formations; significant wildlife habitats; unique scenic or historic areas; wetlands; deserts)
- Renewable resource lands, where development could result in the loss of productivity (e.g., watersheds, aquifers and aquifer-recharge areas, significant agricultural and grazing lands, forest lands)
- Natural hazard lands, where development could endanger life and property (e.g., floodplains, areas with high seismic or volcanic activity, areas of unstable geologic, ice or snow formations)
- Reclamation of lands damaged by surface mining, waste disposal, overgrazing, timber harvesting, farming and other activities
- Acquisition of land for public use
- Identification and regulation of areas impacted by public or private investment where siting results in secondary environmental and socioeconomic impacts
- Review of environmental, social and economic impacts of major public and private developments
- Review of federally funded projects by all government levels
- Conformance of federal land resource activities with approved state programs, particularly where state standards are more stringent than federal standards.

WATER RESOURCES

The League of Women Voters supports:

- Water resource programs and policies that reflect the interrelationships of water quality, water quantity, ground-water and surface water and that address the potential depletion or pollution of water supplies
- Measures to reduce water pollution from direct point-source discharges and from indirect nonpoint sources
- Policies to achieve water quality essential for maintaining species populations and diversity, including measures to protect lakes, estuaries, wetlands and in-stream flows
- Stringent controls to protect the quality of current and potential drinking water supplies, including protection of watersheds for surface supplies and of recharge areas for groundwater.

PROPOSED INTERBASIN WATER TRANSFERS

Interstate and interbasin transfers are not new or unusual. Water transfers have served municipal supplies, industry, energy development and agriculture.

Construction costs of large-scale water transfers are high, and economic losses in the basin of origin also may be high. Environmental costs of water transfers may include quantitative and qualitative changes in wetlands and related fisheries and wildlife, diminished aquifer recharge and reduced stream flows. Lowered water tables also may affect groundwater quality and cause land subsidence.

As we look to the future, water transfer decisions will need to incorporate the high costs of moving water, the limited availability of unallocated water and our still limited knowledge of impacts on the affected ecosystems.

In order to develop member understanding and agreement on proposals for large-scale water transfer projects, state and local Leagues need to work together. The following guidelines are designed to help Leagues jointly evaluate new proposals for large-scale water transfers.

The process for evaluating the suitability of new proposed interbasin water transfers should include:

- Ample and effective opportunities for informed public participation in the formulation and analysis of proposed projects
- Evaluation of economic, social and environmental impacts in the basin of origin, the receiving area and any area through which the diversion must pass, so that decision makers and the public have adequate information on which to base a decision
- Examination of all short- and long-term economic costs including, but not limited to, construction, delivery, operation, maintenance and market interest rate
- Examination of alternative supply options, such as water conservation, water pricing and reclamation
- Participation and review by all affected governments
- Procedures for resolution of inter-governmental conflicts
- Accord with international treaties
- Provisions to ensure that responsibility for funding is borne primarily by the user with no federal subsidy, loan guarantees or use of the borrowing authority of the federal government, unless the proposal is determined by all affected levels of the League to be in the national interest.

WASTE MANAGEMENT

The League of Women Voters supports:

- Policies to reduce the generation and promote the re-use and recycling of solid and hazardous wastes
- Policies to ensure safe treatment, transportation, storage and disposal of solid and hazardous wastes in order to protect public health and air, water and land resources
- Planning and decision making processes that recognize suitable solid and hazardous wastes as potential resources
- Policies for the management of civilian and military high- and low-level radioactive wastes to protect public health, and air, water and land resources
- The establishment of processes for effective involvement of state and local governments and citizens in siting proposals for treatment, storage, disposal and transportation of radioactive wastes
- Full environmental review of treatment, storage and disposal facilities for radioactive wastes

- Safe transport, storage and disposal of radioactive wastes.

CRITERIA FOR SITING WASTE DISPOSAL FACILITIES

The following criteria are derived from the League's Natural Resources positions. They were developed to assist state and local Leagues in reviewing specific waste disposal sites and to help state and local Leagues evaluate both the process employed in site selection and the suitability of a proposed site or hazardous and radioactive waste treatment, storage and disposal facilities. This decision-making process should provide for:

- Ample and effective opportunities for public participation, including funding to conduct such participation
- Evaluation of economic, social and environmental impacts so that decision makers and the public have adequate information on which to base a decision. In addition to the actual site, secondary land use impacts (e.g., buffer areas, adequacy of roads, sewers, water, etc.) should be considered
- An examination of alternative sites and methods of treatment and disposal. Comparison of costs must include short- and long-term costs, such as liability insurance, post closure maintenance, monitoring of ground and surface waters and air before and after closure, and potential loss of land or water resources due to contamination
- Participation and review by all government levels to assure conformance with all adopted comprehensive plans at each level of government
- Procedures for resolution of inter-governmental conflicts.

Hazardous and radioactive waste treatment, storage or disposal facilities should be sited in areas that pose the least amount of risk to the public and to sensitive environmental areas. They should be located away from areas of critical concern such as:

- Natural hazard areas subject to flooding, earthquakes, volcanoes, hurricanes or subsidence
- Drinking water supply sources, such as reservoirs, lakes and rivers and their watersheds, and aquifers and their recharge areas

- Fragile land areas, such as shorelines of rivers, lakes, streams, oceans and estuaries, bays or wetlands
- Rare or valuable ecosystems or geologic formations, significant wildlife habitat or unique scenic or historic areas
- Areas with significant renewable resource value, such as prime agricultural lands or grazing and forest lands that would be destroyed as a result of the siting of hazardous waste facilities
- Residential areas, parks and schools

NUCLEAR ISSUES

The League of Women Voters supports working constructively for the maximum protection of public health and safety and the environment and for citizen participation in the decision-making process at all levels of government.

The League opposes "increased reliance on nuclear fission" but recognizes its place in the nation's energy mix. To achieve this objective:

State and local Leagues may oppose licensing for construction of nuclear power plants on the basis of the national position.

State and local Leagues may oppose licensing for operation of these plants now under construction on a case-by-case basis, after careful consideration of the need for power and of available alternatives and after notifying the national Board.

State and local Leagues may support licensing for construction and operation of nuclear power plants only in special cases and only with prior permission from the national Board.

State and local Leagues may call for the closing of operating nuclear power plants because of specific non-generic health and safety problems, but only with prior permission from the LWVUS.

SITING/STORAGE OF HIGH-LEVEL WASTES (HLWS)

The disposal of HLWs is a national concern, and national policy should govern selection of any facilities constructed, whether an Away-From-Reactor (AFR) interim storage facility, a Monitored Retrievable System (MRS) facility or a permanent geological repository. The Nuclear Waste Policy Act of 1982 sets forth a program for selection, authorization and licensing of permanent repository sites and outlines programs for possible MRS and AFR facilities. In taking any action on this issue, the LWVUS will work to ensure that HLWs are disposed of in a manner that protects public health and safety and the environment.

During the 1981-82 congressional debate over disposal of nuclear wastes, the LWVUS made several statements regarding storage and disposal. The League testified that the storage of HLWs from commercial reactors should be maximized at reactor sites. The League would support a utility-financed AFR facility if one were needed to prevent nuclear power plants from being forced to cease operations because of spent-fuel buildup. In addition, the League supports an active state role in the HLWs decision making process. These concerns, in addition to LWVUS positions on the process and criteria for siting and storage of HLWs, provide the foundation for LWVUS action.

While only a limited number of facilities will probably be built, the LWVUS recognizes that Leagues located in states or communities under consideration as potential sites for such facilities may wish to take action based on national positions. In that event, the state League, or a local League working in concert with the state League, must consult with the LWVUS before taking any action. In making any action determinations on HLWs, the LWVUS will consider three questions:

- Is the proposed facility needed at this time?
- Is the site suitable?
- Did the selection process provide ample and effective opportunities for public participation?

Leagues requesting LWVUS clearance for action should address these questions, particularly the assessment of the suitability of a specific site.

State Leagues also should be alert to action opportunities relating to the process of state consultation and concurrence in the proposed sites.

SITING/STORAGE OF LOW-LEVEL WASTES (LLWS)
The Low-Level Radioactive Waste Policy Act of 1980 makes states responsible for the disposal of LLWs generated at commercial facilities within their borders. The act authorizes states to form regional compacts to establish disposal sites, and it allows states to refuse wastes from other states outside their compact region after January 1, 1986. State legislatures must approve a state's membership in a regional compact, but a compact does not become operational and legally binding until Congress consents to the agreement.

APPROPRIATE STATE LEAGUE ACTION
Some state Leagues are participating in state-level or regional-level discussions/negotiations over regional compacts and are seeking agreement on the compacts. The LWVUS believes it is important for all state Leagues within a proposed compact region to work together to resolve any differences and establish agreement. Clearly, that agreement must be in accord with national positions. Because this is a national concern, the LWVUS must review and approve any agreement reached among state Leagues in a compact region before state Leagues can take any action.

A state League in the proposed compact region that does not support the League agreement cannot act in opposition to that agreement. For example, if a state League disagrees with the approved League agreement, that state League can only lobby its state legislature either to withdraw from the proposed regional compact, i.e., "go it alone," or to join another compact region. A state League also may request LWVUS permission to contact its U.S. senators and representatives at the time Congress considers ratification of the regional compact to lobby them to withdraw the state from the proposed compact. Some individual state Leagues have undertaken studies of proposed compacts for their regions and have reached consensus on a proposed regional compact. Again, that consensus must be in accord with national positions. In addition, before taking any action, the state League must obtain clearance from other state League Boards in the proposed compact region because any action would involve government jurisdictions beyond that League. The state League also should consult the LWVUS before taking action.

A state League or a local League working with the state League can take action on a proposed LLW disposal site based on the public participation process if it concludes the process was inadequate or based on a study of the environmental safety/suitability of the proposed disposal site (see siting criteria). If potential environmental impacts of a proposed site affect more than one League, clearance must be obtained from the relevant League Boards before any action can be taken. If any unresolved differences develop among Leagues, the LWVUS will decide the appropriate course of action.

TRANSPORTATION OF NUCLEAR WASTES

The League recognizes that transporting nuclear wastes increases the likelihood of accidents that could endanger public health. The League also recognizes that transportation is less risky than allowing these wastes to accumulate at an environmentally unsafe facility.

State and local Leagues can work to improve the regulation of transportation of nuclear wastes, but they cannot support "blanket bans" on transporting nuclear wastes through a region or city. There may be instances, however, in which a carefully thought-out ban, based on extensive League study, would be appropriate for a specific area. Such a study should include the overall subject of transporting and managing nuclear wastes, including regulation of types of wastes, packaging, escort, notification of routes to local and state authorities, effective emergency response, and the designating of routes that minimize health, safety and environmental risks. The study should not be confined to one aspect of the transportation issue, such as routes.

If, after a study of the wide-ranging issues involved, a League concludes that wastes should not be transported through an area, that League must discuss the results of the study and obtain clearance for any contemplated action from all appropriate levels of the League.

DEFENSE WASTES

In managing high-level nuclear wastes, the League supports equivalent treatment of civilian and military wastes. The League supports the state consultation and concurrence process, consideration of environmental impacts of proposed sites and NRC licensing for defense waste facilities as

well as for civilian waste facilities. The League's position on equivalent treatment of all wastes includes transportation of defense wastes. Low-level defense wastes include wastes from military medical programs, naval shipyards that maintain nuclear-powered naval vessels and research facilities. The treatment of low-level defense wastes, however, is not spelled out in the Low-level Waste Policy Act of 1980. Most low-level defense wastes are disposed of in special federal facilities; however, some are disposed of in existing commercial sites.

Leagues may take the same action on transporting, siting and storing defense wastes as on civilian wastes. Action on defense wastes should be in accordance with any relevant future National Security positions developed by the League.

INTER-LEAGUE COOPERATION

Leagues contemplating action on nuclear waste issues should keep in mind that any action almost invariably will affect areas beyond their jurisdiction. Thus, in all cases, local Leagues should clear action with the state League and the League Boards at the appropriate jurisdictional levels.

One example of necessary inter-League action on a regional level is the low-level radioactive waste compacting process. The League believes this is an important national, state and local concern aimed at responsible management and disposal of low-level wastes. Many state Leagues are actively participating in their regional processes, and some are taking consensus on the issue.

PUBLIC PARTICIPATION

While fighting for a broad range of environmental legislation, the League has stressed citizen participation as a necessary component of decision-making at all levels of government.

In pressing for full implementation of the Clean Air Act of 1970, the League fought for greater citizen access to state plans for achieving national ambient air-quality standards. League efforts to educate and involve the public in waste management issues at the state and local levels have included support for mandatory beverage container deposit legislation, known as "bottle bills," to promote recycling and reuse. In supporting the Nuclear Waste Policy Act of 1982, Leagues pushed for adequate state consultation and concurrence in nuclear waste repository siting decisions. In statements to the nuclear regulatory community, state Leagues emphasized the need for citizen participation in nuclear power decisions.

League efforts to promote household hazardous waste collection across the country, to ensure safe drinking water for all and to protect groundwater also are all part of a continuing focus on heightening citizen awareness and participation in decision making.

Passage of the Emergency Planning and Community Right-to-Know Act of 1986 (SARA Title III) gave Leagues a new tool to combat pollution. This act gives communities access to information from chemical facilities on releases and spills, allows "regulation by information" and encourages the development of emergency response plans and strong pollution prevention measures by industry. During the 1990s, the League continued the fight, advocating expansion of community right-to-know provisions in the renewal of the Resource Conservation and Recovery Act (RCRA). It was also successful in defeating congressional efforts to pass "regulatory reform" legislation aimed at crippling the adoption and enforcement of environmental protection regulations.

In 1996, the League joined 24 public interest organizations in supporting the President's move to phase out the use of methyl bromide, an extremely toxic pesticide. Also, the LWVUS and 84 national, international and local organizations jointly urged Congress to cosponsor the Children's Environmental Protection Act of 1997 (CEPA), which sought to ensure a citizen's right to know if there are harmful toxicants in the environment.

In 1996, the Department of Energy asked the LWVEF to help develop a National Dialogue on Nuclear Materials and Waste Management. Pilot field workshops were held in 1997, but the Dialogue was opposed by some environmen-

talists and state officials. The LWVEF held two intersite discussions in San Diego and Chicago on nuclear material and waste in 1998 and issued a report.

THE LEAGUE'S POSITION

The League of Women Voters believes public understanding and cooperation are essential to the responsible and responsive management of our nation's natural resources. The public has a right to know about pollution levels, dangers to health and the environment, and proposed resource management policies and options. The public has a right to participate in decision-making at each phase in the process and at each level of government involvement. Officials should make a special effort to develop readily understandable procedures for public involvement and to ensure that the public has adequate information to participate effectively. Public records should be readily accessible at all governmental levels. Adequate funding is needed to ensure opportunities for public education and effective public participation in all aspects of the decision-making process.

The appropriate level of government should publicize, in an extensive and timely manner and in readily available sources, information about pollution levels, pollution-abatement programs, and resource management policies and options. Hearings should be held in easily accessible locations, at convenient times and, when possible, in the area concerned. The hearing procedures and other opportunities for public comment should actively encourage citizen participation in decision-making.

The League supports public education that provides a basic understanding of the environment and the social, economic and environmental costs and benefits of environmental protection, pollution control and conservation.

Mechanisms for citizen appeal must be guaranteed, including access to the courts. Due process rights for the affected public and private parties must be assured.

AGRICULTURE POLICIES

In 1986, the League undertook a two-year study and member agreement process on the role of the federal government in U.S. agriculture policy, examining elements of federal farm policy, and its contemporary setting and policy alternatives. The resulting 1988 position on agriculture policy supports policies for sustainable agriculture and action to reduce the use of toxic chemicals on the farm. The League also supports targeting research programs and technological assistance to mid-sized farms and to sustainable agriculture. While many of the programs the League supports, such as farm credit at reasonable terms and conditions and programs to enable farmers to use sustainable agriculture, may benefit family or mid-sized farms, the League supports these programs for all farms, regardless of size.

The position supports "decoupling" (moving away from direct payments based on production) as consistent with the strong League consensus in favor of greater reliance on the free market to determine prices. Reliance on the free market for price determination also can support a gradual reduction in loan rates. The League does not envision total reliance on the free market to determine agriculture prices. In assessing programs that move agriculture toward greater reliance on the free market, consideration would include problems peculiar to agriculture, such as severe climate or natural disasters.

The League supports federally-provided farm credit, but believes the federal government should be the lender of last resort. The League position does not address supply controls, capping payments to farmers, protecting farm income or any particular commodity program. It supports the conservation reserve program and opposes the removal of lands prematurely from the conservation reserve.

In 1989, the League opposed federal legislation that would have preempted stricter state laws on the regulation of pesticides. In 1990, it urged the House to pass a farm bill that would protect land and water resources, reduce the use of toxic chemicals, and target research and technical assistance to developing environmentally sound agriculture practices. The League called for measures to strengthen conservation provisions, continue the conservation reserve, and permit retention of base payments and deficiency payments when farmers file and implement an approved plan for farming with environmentally beneficial practices. The League also called for national standards of organic production and opposed the export of pesticides that are illegal in the United States. In 1988-1991, the LWVEF worked with Public Voice for Food and Health Policy and state and local Leagues on a citizen education project on agricultural issues, including pesticide residues in food and water, sustainable agriculture, and research and technology.

At Convention 2012, delegates voted to review and update the LWV Agriculture position. A study committee was appointed and in 2014, Leagues reached member agreement on a new position which was announced in May 2014.

THE LEAGUE'S POSITION

The League Women Voters believes federal agriculture policies should promote adequate supplies of food and fiber at reasonable prices to consumers, farms that are economically viable, farm practices that are environmentally sound and increased reliance on the free market to determine prices.

SUSTAINABLE AGRICULTURE

Federal policy should encourage a system of sustainable, regenerative agricultural production that moves toward an environmentally sound agricultural sector. This includes promoting stewardship to preserve and protect the country's human and natural agricultural resources.

RESEARCH AND DEVELOPMENT

Agricultural research, development and technical assistance should continue to be a major federal function. Resources should be targeted to developing sustainable agricultural practices and addressing the needs of mid-size farms.

AGRICULTURE AND TRADE

U.S. efforts should be directed toward expanding export markets for our agricultural products while mini-

mizing negative effects on developing nations' economies. Consistent with the League's trade position, multilateral trade negotiations should be used to reduce other countries' barriers and/or subsidies protecting their agricultural products.

AGRICULTURAL PRICES

The LWVUS supports an increasing reliance on the free market to determine the price of agricultural commodities and the production decisions of farmers, in preference to traditional price support mechanisms.

FARM CREDIT

Farmers should have access to credit with reasonable terms and conditions. Federally provided farm credit is essential to maintaining the viability of farm operations when the private sector is unable or unwilling to provide the credit farmers need.

Of these policies, the League believes the most essential for the future of agriculture are:

- Encouraging sustainable agriculture
- Providing research, information and technical assistance to agricultural producers
- Increasing reliance on the free market to determine prices.

Statement of Position on Federal Agriculture Policy, as Announced by National Board, October 1988.

The League Women Voters believes government should provide financial support for agriculture that includes disaster assistance, crop insurance, need-based loans and incentives to adopt best management practices. Support should be extended to specialty crops, such as fruits, vegetables and nuts; to new production methods, such as organic, hydroponic, and urban practices; and to farms that supply local and regional markets.

Subsidized crop yield insurance should be linked to implementation of best management practices with the subsidy denied for marginal or environmentally sensitive land. The premium subsidy for crop insurance should be available for a wide range of crops, such as fruits, vegetables and specialty crops. Government should limit the amount of the premium subsidy received by larger farms.

The League supports policies that increase competition in agricultural markets. Antitrust laws should be enforced to ensure competitive agricultural markets. Alternative marketing systems such as regional hub markets, farmers' markets and farmers' cooperatives should be promoted.

Clean air and water regulations should apply to all animal and aquaculture production and processing facilities, and not just to the very large confined animal feeding operations (CAFOs). Such regulations should be designed in a manner that takes into account environmentally sound technologies and the scale of the operation being regulated. Small size operations should not be granted automatic exemption from regulation.

The League believes that government regulatory agencies dealing with animal and aquaculture production should have adequate authority and funding to:

- Enforce regulations
- Gather information that supports monitoring the impacts of all animal feeding and aquaculture operations on human and animal health and the environment.

Government should fund basic research related to agriculture. Government funded research should also address the impact of new technologies on human health and the environment prior to widespread adoption of products developed with such technologies. Assessment of products developed with new technologies should be conducted as transparently as possible, while respecting intellectual property rights. Research should be funded to support the continuation of diversified and sustainable agricultural systems, such as seed banking and promoting and preserving genetic diversity.

To provide adequate safety of our food supply, government should:

- Clarify and enforce pre-market testing requirements for foods and food additives developed using any new chemical technology, such as genetic engineering or nanotechnology
- Require developers to monitor all such new food products developed after releasing to the market
- Require developers of such new food products to provide data and other materials to independent third parties for pre- and post-marketing safety assessment
- Fund independent third party risk assessment examining how long term and multiple exposures to such new foods affect human health and the environment
- Withdraw marketing approval and require recall if such products are shown to be unsafe
- Require post-market monitoring of human health and environmental impacts for pharmaceutical applications used in animal and aquaculture production
- Limit use of antibiotics in animal production to the treatment of disease
- Promote crop management practices that decrease dependency on added chemicals
- Fund, employ and train sufficient personnel for assessment and compliance functions of regulatory agencies.

The League supports government developing and requiring more informative and standardized definitions on product labeling. Food labeling and advertising should display only approved health and safety claims and an accurate representation of the required ingredient and nutrition lists. The League supports consumer education about labeling of foods developed using any new technology.

Statement of Position on Federal Agriculture Policies as Announced by the National Board, May 2014.

SOCIAL POLICY

Secure equal rights and equal opportunity for all. Promote social and economic justice, and the health and safety of all Americans.

From its inception, the League has worked for equal rights and social reforms. In the early years, the League was one of the first organizations to address such issues as child welfare, maternal and child health programs, child labor protection and laws that discriminated against women.

In the 1960s, with the nation's unrest over civil rights, the League began building a foundation of support for equal access to education, employment and housing. The fight against discrimination broadened in the 1970s and 1980s, and the League supported the Equal Rights Amendment (ERA) in 1972, fighting hard for ratification by the states. As that effort fell short, support for the ERA undergirded action on issues from pay equity to Title IX, which required equal educational opportunity for women.

Based on 1970s work to combat poverty and discrimination, a two-year study evaluating public and private responsibilities for providing food, shelter and a basic income level ended in 1988 and culminated in a position on Meeting Basic Human Needs. Programs to increase the availability and quality of child care and protect children at risk remained a concern.

In the 1980s, fiscal issues, from tax reform to entitlement programs and deficit reduction, were at the forefront of the League program. The League was a major force in the tax-reform effort to eliminate loopholes and promote fairness. It sought deficit reduction while protecting federal old-age, survivors, disability and health insurance.

In the late 1980s and early 1990s, the League worked to increase the availability of quality child care and adopted a position in favor of community and government programs to help children reach their full potential, including early childhood education.

Leagues nationwide also work hard on transportation issues, focusing on environmental protection and ensuring the availability of public transportation for access to employment and housing.

In the 1990s, concern for violence prevention spurred a new League position and brought strong support for commonsense measures to control gun violence. The League supported the Brady bill and sought to close loopholes that undermine consumer safety.

The 2006 Convention voted to undertake a study on immigration. After study and consensus, the new position was finalized in 2008 and sent to Capitol Hill.

Given the growing crisis in health care delivery and financing in the 1990s, the League developed a comprehensive position supporting a health care system that provides access to affordable, quality health care for all Americans and protects patients' rights. In 2010, the League's efforts saw success when the Affordable Care Act (ACA) was signed into law. Throughout the 112th Congress, the League continued to defend the ACA from challenges in Congress and the courts.

At Convention 2010, delegates voted to study the role of the Federal Government in Public Education and, in March 2012, the Board announced a new position. Delegates to Convention 2012 adopted by concurrence a new position on Sentencing Equality.

The League's position on Human Trafficking was adopted by concurrence at Convention 2014.

EQUALITY OF OPPORTUNITY

By 1966, the League had reached its first position on combatting poverty and discrimination: support of policies and programs to provide equal opportunity for all in education and employment. The position described general criteria and specific kinds of programs to further these goals.

"An evaluation of equality of opportunity for housing" was in the proposed program slated for 1968 Convention consideration. Two events that spring caused delegates to alter the normal sequence of study/consensus/position: the shock waves in cities following the assassination of Dr. Martin Luther King, Jr., and the passage of a new civil rights bill that included fair housing.

Convinced that League members knew where they stood on fair housing, delegates amended the existing position at Convention, adding support for equality of opportunity for housing. And they redirected the study from an evaluation of the concept to an evaluation of the means to achieve the goal. By December 1969, members had endorsed criteria for ensuring fair housing and adequate housing supply.

The League has consistently supported federal programs aimed at combating poverty and discrimination and has worked at the community level for successful implementation. The list is long, starting with programs initiated under the long-defunct Office of Economic Opportunity (OEO), legal services, community action agencies, Job Corps, urban renewal, Model Cities and other programs designed to provide equal access to housing, employment and education.

When the federal government combined many categorical grant programs into block grants, the League found new ways to work for the goals and policies it supports. In 1973, the League began monitoring the impact of the General Revenue Sharing (GRS) program on poverty and discrimination. This resulted in reforms incorporated into the 1976 GRS amendments that tightened weak antidiscrimination provisions and expanded citizen participation and accountability requirements. But efforts to direct more funds to jurisdictions in greatest need failed.

Since the late 1970s, threats to League goals and policies have taken the form of frequent legislative and executive attempts to drastically reduce federal funding of League-supported programs, as well as persistent moves to dilute existing civil rights laws and policies. The League has actively opposed tuition tax credits, budget cuts in social welfare programs and large, untargeted block grants. At the same time the League has supported strengthened fair-housing legislation and civil rights legislation to reaffirm congressional intent in passing Title IX of the Education Amendments of 1972, that the law be broadly interpreted and applied.

The League's Social Policy positions were revised in 1989. The Equal Access to Education, Employment, and Housing position was combined with Equal Rights into one Equality of Opportunity position.

The 1992 Convention added language to the Equality of Opportunity position, stating that it referred to "all persons, regardless of their race, color, gender, religion, national origin, age, sexual orientation or disability." In July 1992, the LWVUS joined the National Endorsement Campaign in calling for the extension of existing civil rights laws by local, state and federal legislation to prohibit discrimination against lesbians and gay men in jobs, housing and public accommodations. In the 106th Congress, the LWVUS supported federal legislation targeting hate crimes. Convention 2010 added language to the Equality of Opportunity position to equalize the rights of same-gender couples to those of heterosexual couples.

Education

INTEGRATION

The League is committed to racial integration of schools as a necessary condition for equal access to education.

When busing became one means of achieving school desegregation, Leagues worked to ensure that laws were obeyed peacefully by building coalitions, running rumor-control centers, sometimes going to court to get compliance. At the national level, the League worked to oppose antibusing/anti-desegregation initiatives in Congress.

The League served as an *amicus* in Supreme Court challenges to the desegregation process. The LWVEF maintained a desegregation clearinghouse and assembled League leaders and national policy experts for a workshop on metropolitan school desegregation in 1982-1984.

QUALITY EDUCATION

The 1974-1976 LWVUS Program included the phrase "equal access to...quality education," reflecting League recognition that "equality" and "quality" are inseparable. However, the LWVUS has never undertaken a process for determining a common League definition of quality education that could serve as a basis for action nationwide. Therefore, when the definition of quality is a key factor in a state or local community, a local or state League must conduct its own study rather than relying on the LWVUS position to take action. Many Leagues that have member agreement on quality education in specific terms use their positions to support an array of local and state educational reforms. A number of Leagues have used this position to oppose private school vouchers. The LWVUS is a member of the National Coalition for Public Education, which opposes vouchers.

TUITION TAX CREDITS

The 1978 Convention directed the national board to oppose tax credits for families of children attending private elementary and secondary schools. Convention action was based on League support for equal access to education and support for desegregation as a means of promoting equal access. The League is concerned about the negative impact that tuition tax credits would have on the public schools by encouraging flight, particularly from desegregated schools. The League also supports federal efforts through Internal Revenue Service (IRS) regulation to deny tax-exempt status to racially discriminatory "segregation academies."

FEDERAL PROGRAMS

The League supports many federal education programs, some designed to meet the special educational needs of the poor and minorities and others to give women and minorities equal education opportunities.

The League worked for passage of Title IX of the Education Amendments of 1972, which prohibits sex discrimination in educational institutions that receive federal aid. Subsequently, the League has focused on thwarting congressional attempts to dilute Title IX, as well as on advancing federal enforcement efforts. At the national level, the League was active in major court challenges to Title IX, defending key provisions and urging a broad interpretation of the scope of Title IX. In 1983, the League filed an *amicus* brief in *Grove City College v. Bell*, a major Supreme Court case that narrowed considerably the prohibitions of Title IX. In 1984, after the Court's decision, the League supported efforts in Congress for new legislation clarifying congressional intent on the scope of coverage of Title IX and similar civil rights statutes.

In 2003, the League responded to a Department of Education effort to scale back Title IX. The LWVUS opposed attempts to weaken the law and lobbied in support of congressional resolutions affirming that Title IX had made great progress in establishing equal opportunity for girls and women in education and in school athletics. In July 2003, the Department of Education affirmed its support for Title IX without change. In September 2004, the LWVUS signed on to an *amicus* brief in *Jackson v. Birmingham Board of Education*, supporting the original intent of Title IX of broad and effective protection against gender discrimination by ensuring that individuals who bring discriminatory practices to light are protected from retaliation and reprisal.

Under an LWVEF project to monitor sex equity in vocational education programs in 1981-1982, several state Leagues evaluated progress toward meeting federal sex-equity mandates. Vocational education programs have significant impact on employment, particularly for women who have difficulty gaining access to training programs for higher paying jobs. In addition, the League promoted the enrollment of girls and young women in math and science courses to prepare them for the jobs of the future.

EDUCATION FINANCING

Many state and local Leagues have identified inequities in education financing during the course of their own program studies and have worked for reforms. Action on school financing equity takes place predominantly at the state level, where school financing laws are made.

Employment

The League has supported federal job training programs and is on record in favor of a full employment policy, i.e., the concept of assuring a job for all those able and seeking to work. In 1978, the League supported passage of the Humphrey-Hawkins bill to promote full employment.

The League supported the public service employment (PSE) component of the Comprehensive Employment and Training Program (CETA) during the 1970s and worked for the passage of emergency jobs legislation in 1983, spearheading a Call to Action for Jobs for Women that resulted in more funding for the types of public-service jobs that women traditionally perform. In 1994, the League unsuccessfully supported passage of the Infrastructure Jobs Act and the Full Employment Opportunity Act, both targeted especially to urban areas.

Nondiscrimination & Affirmative Action

Through legislative and regulatory approaches, as well as litigation, the League advocates affirmative action programs for minorities and women. Action has included a lawsuit to compel the U.S. Department of Labor (DOL) to issue goals and timetables governing the employment of women in nontraditional jobs and apprenticeship programs and prodding to ensure enforcement. The League has worked to combat administrative initiatives to restrict the enforcement authority of DOL's Office of Federal Contract Compliance Programs (OFCCP) and the Equal Employment Opportunity Commission (EEOC). Since 1977, the League has supported measures to combat employment discrimination in Congress itself.

The League has been outspoken in supporting affirmative action programs and policies. That support has included filing *amicus* briefs in key affirmative action lawsuits, including *Kaiser Aluminum and Chemical Corp. v. Weber* in 1979, *Boston Firefighters Union, Local 718 v. Boston Chapter NAACP* in 1983, *Firefighters Local Union No. 1784 v. Stotts* in 1984 and *Williams v. City of New Orleans* in 1983. The League has actively opposed attempts by OFCCP to weaken regulations that govern the federal contract compliance program. During the 1985-1986 Supreme Court term, the League filed *amicus* briefs in three key affirmative action cases: *Local 28 Sheet Metal Workers v. EEOC, Local 93 International Association of Firefighters v. City of Cleveland*, and *Wygant v. Jackson Board of Education*. The Court reaffirmed the validity of voluntary race-based affirmative action in these cases.

In 1986, the LWVUS signed onto another *amicus* brief filed in the U.S. Supreme Court, *Johnson v. Transportation Agency*. In 1987, the Court held that public employers may adopt voluntary affirmative action plans to attain work force balances in traditionally segregated job categories. This was the first instance in which the Supreme Court upheld a gender-based affirmative action plan.

In 1988, the League participated in a Supreme Court *amicus* brief in *Patterson v. McLean Credit Union*. In its 1989 decision, the Court reaffirmed that Section 1981 of the Civil Rights Act of 1986, which prohibits racial discrimination in contracts, applies to private acts of discrimination. However, the Court also held that Section 1981 does not apply to racial harassment or other discriminatory working conditions that arise after an employment contract has been entered into.

Between 1984 and 1988, the League was an active player in successfully urging Congress to pass the Civil Rights Restoration Act, which restored four anti-discrimination laws that were narrowed by the Supreme Court's 1984 *Grove City v. Bell* decision. Subsequently, the League endorsed the Civil Rights Act, which reversed a series of 1989 Supreme Court decisions that seriously weakened federal employment discrimination laws, and strengthened protections under federal civil rights laws. In 1990, the bill passed both Houses of Congress but was vetoed by the President. In 1991 a compromise bill was passed by Congress and signed by the President. The League did not actively support this bill, in part because it placed a monetary limit on damages for sex discrimination, including sexual harassment. In 1992, the League joined other groups in supporting the Equal Remedies Act, which would remove the monetary limit on damages in civil rights laws.

In response to continued congressional attacks, the League joined other concerned organizations in the Leadership Conference on Civil Rights (LCCR) to reaffirm strong support for affirmative action programs.

In 2004 and 2006, the League opposed the "Federal Marriage Amendment," which would permanently write discrimination into the United States Constitution by limiting fundamental protections such as health care benefits for same-sex partners.

In 2008, the League joined other organizations in support of the Americans with Disabilities Act (ADA) Amendments Act of 2008 (ADAAA), designed to restore the ADA to its original intent and ensure coverage for disabled Americans in all aspects of society. The bill was passed and signed into law. In 2012, the League joined an *amicus* brief in an affirmative action case before the Supreme Court, urging the Court to recognize that diversity in higher education is crucial for the success of our multi-racial democracy.

Pay Equity

League work on pay equity (equal pay for jobs of comparable worth) stemmed from member concern over the feminization of poverty. The League played a key role at the national level through its work with the broad-based National Committee on Pay Equity in the 1980s. In 1986, the LWVEF participated in an *amicus* brief before the U.S. Supreme Court in the pay equity case, *Bazemore v. Friday*. The Court ruled a state agency may be held liable for disparities in salaries between blacks and whites, even if the disparities were caused by racial discrimination that occurred before the 1964 Civil Rights Act.

State and local Leagues also have endorsed legislative efforts to undertake job evaluation studies or to implement pay equity for public employees.

Fair Housing

The League made passage of the Fair Housing Amendments a priority in 1980. The legislation passed the House but was filibustered in the Senate. Another attempt in 1983-1984 was put on hold in light of more pressing civil rights issues. The League also supported reauthorization of the Home Mortgage Disclosure Act (HMDA) in 1982.

LWVEF participation in a Department of Housing and Urban Development (HUD)-funded project in 1979-1981 enabled local Leagues to promote the entry of women into the mortgage credit market and sparked interest in the problems of single-headed households, displaced homemakers and discrimination against families with children. Also in the 1980s, LWV supported prohibitions on housing discrimination against families with children.

In 2005, the League urged Congress to create the Affordable Housing Fund, a long overdue step toward addressing the housing crisis that confronts very low- and extremely low-income families. It also urged House members to protect activities of the nonprofit groups providing the bulk of housing services for our poorest communities.

Equal Rights

In 1972, shortly after congressional passage of the Equal Rights Amendment (ERA), the national Convention overwhelmingly approved support of "equal rights for all regardless of sex" as a necessary extension of the League's long-term support for equal opportunity for all. Delegates also voted to support the ERA. With this decisive action, the League came full circle in giving priority support once again to equal rights for women and men.

The foremothers of the women's movement, in their 1848 Conventions at Seneca Falls and Rochester, New York, rooted the movement in a demand for women's equality before the law. The right to vote came to be seen as the key that would unlock the door to the others. This vision sustained the National American Woman Suffrage Association (NAWSA), the forerunner of the League.

When the 19th Amendment was passed in 1920, suffrage leaders divided on strategy. Some founded the National Woman's Party, which sponsored the first ERA, introduced in Congress in 1923. Others, the founders of the League among them, decided not to push for an ERA. It is hard for League members now to imagine the time in which the League actually opposed the ERA. It was not for lack of concern for women's rights. The League's record on that point speaks for itself. Rather, it was a problem in priorities. At the League's 1921 Convention, delegates decided that an ERA might adversely affect new and hard-won state labor legislation, which offered some protection to tens of thousands of women working in nonunionized, unskilled jobs.

Moreover, though it was an organization of women, the early League wanted to affirm strongly that its interests and lobbying activities were not confined to women's issues. The League in the 1920s and 1930s set the stage for future program development by focusing on a broad range of social issues. Many were, of course, of obvious concern for women: the Sheppard-Towner Act, which provided for federally funded infant and maternity care; the removal of discrimination against women in immigration and naturalization laws; equality for women in the Civil Service Classification Act; equal pay for equal work. During the same period, local and state Leagues worked to eliminate sex discrimination affecting jury duty, property rights, the treatment of women offenders and a number of other issues.

Through the 1940s, the national League program included "removal of legal and administrative discriminations against women," but retained the statement in opposition to an ERA until 1954 when the national program was restructured and it disappeared.

As the League became active in the civil rights struggle of the 1960s, members grew acutely aware of the parallels between the status of women and minorities. Many state and local Leagues pursued women's issues with new vigor, and a strong push for women's issues developed at the national level, culminating in the 1972 Convention action.

Subsequent Conventions have reaffirmed the League's commitment to the ERA. The 1980 Convention took the League's commitment a step further, voting to use the existing ERA position as a basis not only for ratification efforts, but also to work on gender-based discrimination through action to bring laws into compliance with the goals of the ERA.

In 1972, lobbying for ratification and against rescission on a state-by-state basis became a top League priority at the national and state levels.

In 1979, the LWVUS organized the National Business Council (NBC) for ERA, the first formal structure to bring major business leaders into the fight for ratification. In 1981, under an LWVUS/NBC partnership, a volunteer task force of advertising executives developed and produced radio ads designed to "sell" the ERA in seven unratified states. Throughout the media campaign, the LWVUS provided extensive technical and financial assistance to state Leagues and ERA coalitions, and worked to organize business efforts in the states.

The ratification process was not completed by the June 30, 1982, deadline, but the League's support of a constitutional guarantee of equal protection under the law remains strong. The League supported reintroduction of the ERA in Congress in 1982 and helped lead a lobbying effort that culminated in a narrow November 1983 defeat in the House.

In July 1993, the League signed on to an *amicus* brief in the Supreme Court case, *J.E.B. v. T.B*, which argued that sex discrimination in jury selection is prohibited by the Equal Protection Clause of the 14th Amendment. League participation was based on support for actions to bring laws into compliance with the ERA. In 1994, the Supreme Court agreed, ruling that state laws allowing jury challenges based solely on sex are unconstitutional.

The League will continue to work to achieve the goals of the expanded ERA position. Issues cover action for pay equity and support for the Economic Equity Act, which includes provisions to eliminate sex discrimination in pensions and insurance. In 1996, the League endorsed the Women's Pension Equity Act, legislation designed to make pension law simpler and more even-handed. Meanwhile, the League continues to lay the groundwork for passage and ratification of the ERA.

On the international front, the League of Women Voters supports the United Nations Convention for the Elimination of All Forms of Discrimination against Women (CEDAW) and is on the Steering Committee of the NGO

UNICEF Working Group on Girls at the UN, which formed an International Network for Girls, a global advocacy network.

THE LEAGUE'S POSITION

The League of Women Voters believes that the federal government shares with other levels of government the responsibility to provide equality of opportunity for education, employment and housing for all persons in the United States regardless of their race, color, gender, religion, national origin, age, sexual orientation or disability. Employment opportunities in modern, technological societies are closely related to education; therefore, the League supports federal programs to increase the education and training of disadvantaged people. The League supports federal efforts to prevent and/or remove discrimination in education, employment and housing and to help communities bring about racial integration of their school systems.

The League of Women Voters of the United States supports equal rights for all regardless of sex. The League supports action to bring laws into compliance with the ERA:

- To eliminate or amend those laws that have the effect of discriminating on the basis of sex
- To promote laws that support the goals of the ERA
- To strengthen the enforcement of such existing laws.

The League of Women Voters of the United States supports equal rights for all under state and federal law. LWVUS supports legislation to equalize the legal rights, obligations, and benefits available to same-gender couples with those available to heterosexual couples. LWVUS supports legislation to permit same-gender couples to marry under civil law. The League believes that the civil status of marriage is already clearly distinguished from the religious institution of marriage and that religious rights will be preserved.

Statement of Position on Equality of Opportunity, as Revised by the National Board in January 1989, based on Positions Announced by the National Board in January 1969, adopted by the 1972 Convention, Expanded by the 1980 Convention and the 2010 Convention.

FURTHER GUIDANCE AND CRITERIA

In more specific terms, the kinds of programs the League supports include:

- Programs in basic education, occupational education and retraining when needed at any point of an individual's working career
- Expanded opportunities in apprenticeship and on-the-job training programs
- Child-care centers for preschool children to give parents the opportunity for employment
- Greatly increased educational opportunity through compensatory programs for disadvantaged groups beginning at the preschool level and extending through secondary education
- Federal financial aid to help needy students remain in high school and to take advantage of post-high school training and education
- A regional approach to problems of economically depressed areas that cuts across state lines. This approach can be handled administratively by such means as interstate cooperation or more formal interstate compacts or commissions made up of representatives of state and federal governments. Development programs should reflect the needs of the particular area and can include such measures as provision of education and training for available jobs, encouragement of new industry in the area, development and conservation of natural resources and the building of public facilities.
- Programs that would inform individuals of their civil rights in education, employment and housing, and of the opportunities open to them
- Full use of mediation and conciliation in efforts to bring about integration of minority groups into full participation in community life

- A federal clearinghouse for the exchange of information on solutions communities have found to problems of integration in employment, education and housing
- Programs to bring about effective integration of schools through federal technical assistance such as training programs and institutes for teachers and school administrators
- Withholding federal funds from school districts that fail to meet realistic and effective guidelines and standards for school integration
- Withholding government contracts from businesses and industries that discriminate in employment
- An effective federal fair employment practices agency.

EDUCATION AND EMPLOYMENT CRITERIA

In evaluating federal programs that have been, or will be, established to provide equality of opportunity for education and employment, the League will support those programs that largely fulfill the following criteria:

- The nationwide effort to achieve equality of opportunity in education and employment should include participation of government at all levels and encourage the participation of private institutions.
- State and local governments should contribute to the extent their resources permit. At the same time, adequate federal funds for the establishment and continuation of programs should be available if necessary.
- Programs should be carefully tailored to the educational or employment needs of the people they are intended to reach.
- People for whom community action programs are designed should be involved in the planning and implementation of those programs.
- The programs should be carried out by personnel competent to meet the specific requirements of their jobs.
- Programs should assist people to become self-supporting, contributing members of society.
- The programs should be nondiscriminatory with provisions for enforcement.
- Research, pilot projects and continuing evaluation should be encouraged and, where feasible, built into programs.

- Programs may be closely related but should avoid unnecessary duplication.

FAIR HOUSING CRITERIA

The following criteria should be applied to programs and policies to provide equal opportunity for access to housing without discrimination:

- Opportunities for purchase or renting of homes and for borrowing money for housing should not be restricted because of discriminatory reasons such as race, color, sex, religion or national origin.
- Responsibility in the nationwide effort to achieve equality of opportunity for access to housing resides with government at all levels and with the private sector—builders, lending institutions, realtors, labor unions, business and industry, news media, civic organizations, educational institutions, churches and private citizens.
- The continued existence of patterns of discrimination depends on the covert support of community leaders, institutions and residents. Award or withdrawal of federal contracts and placement of federal installations should be used as levers to change this covert support.
- After positive steps, such as mediation and conciliation have been exhausted, the federal government should have the option for selective withholding of federal funds where patterns of discrimination in access to housing occur. In applying the option to withhold funds, the federal government should weigh the effects of its actions on the welfare of lower-income and minority groups.
- Federal programs should include provisions to guarantee equal opportunity for access to housing. Federal funds should not be used to perpetuate discrimination.
- In the enforcement of fair-housing laws, speedy resolution should be ensured. Administrative procedures and responsibilities should be clearly defined and widely publicized.
- Mediation and legal redress should be readily available. The process should ensure every possible protection for both complainant and persons or institutions against whom complaints are lodged. Avenues for mediation and legal redress should be widely publicized and should be easily accessible.

- Funding should be adequate to provide trained and competent staff for public education to inform citizens of the provisions of fair-housing legislation, of their fair-housing rights and of procedures to be followed in securing them. Adequate funding should also be available for mediation and for all aspects of speedy enforcement.
- There should be continued evaluation to provide a basis for revision and strengthening of all procedures so that equality of opportunity for access to housing can be accomplished.

FEDERAL ROLE IN PUBLIC EDUCATION

Convention 2010 delegates voted to embark on a two-year study of the Federal Role in Public Education. Local and state Leagues across the country participated in the study and a position was announced in March 2012.

THE LEAGUE'S POSITION

The League of Women Voters believes that the federal government shares with other levels of government the responsibility to provide an equitable, quality public education for all children pre-K through grade 12. A quality public education is essential for a strong, viable, and sustainable democratic society and is a civil right.

The League believes that the role of the federal government should include the following:

- Provide leadership and vision to promote a quality education for all children
- Provide broad common standards developed by educational experts upon which states and local education agencies can build
- Provide a suggested curricular structure or framework as a guide to state and local education agencies to develop their own curricula

- Provide a national assessment that clearly informs teachers, parents and students about how well individual students have mastered criteria established at the national level
- Provide a national assessment that informs districts how well their populations compare to other populations similar to theirs
- Provide a combination of competitive grants and non-competitive funding to states and local school districts to achieve equity among states and populations.

The League of Women Voters believes that an equitable, quality public education is critical for students. While the League recognizes that there are instances where the federal government's involvement is the only way to achieve universal change (desegregation, special needs population, gender equity), we also recognize that primary responsibility for public education resides with the states. In accordance with the League of Women Voters' position on Equal Rights, the League continues to support equity in public education for all through:

- Broad guidelines for accountability, leaving implementation to the state and local education agencies
- Adequate funding sources that support the broad goals of national standards
- Mechanisms for local and state funding with adequate federal support for mandates that require less burdensome, compliance-based reporting and regulations.

The League of Women Voters believes a basic role of the federal government in funding education should be to achieve equity among states and populations on the basis of identified needs. This should be done with full understanding that equity does not mean equal, given that some populations are more expensive to educate than others and some localities have specific needs.

The League believes that the federal government should be primarily responsible for funding any programs mandated by the federal government on local education agencies. Although the League recognizes equity in education depends on meeting basic human needs of children and of their families, the costs associated with providing equitable access to safe neighborhoods and secure housing do not belong in the education budget. Major programs of federal funding for public education (i.e., Elementary and Secondary Education Act) should be targeted toward children living in poverty and/or children with special needs.

The federal government has the responsibility to monitor and support access to the following:

- High quality teaching and learning, supported by quality current learning materials and well maintained educational facilities
- Access to health care needs (i.e., hearing, vision, dental, immunization, school-based health clinics at the secondary level, etc.) and nutritionally adequate food (i.e., school-based meals under "free and reduced meal programs").

The League believes that the first five years of a child's life are crucial in building the foundation for educational attainment and greatly impact success or failure in later life. Additionally, the League believes quality, developmentally appropriate and voluntary early learning experiences should be available to all children, with federally funded opportunities going first to children of poverty and/or with special needs. The League believes that the federal government should support the following:

- Early childhood education programs that include funding for parent education and involve child development, health, nutrition and access to other supportive services, such as mental health care for all children and their families
- Research that documents quality early childhood education programs
- Research that demonstrates the importance of linking state and local community partnerships with effective early childhood education programs and services.

Statement of Position on Federal Role in Public Education as announced by the National Board in March 2012.

FISCAL POLICY

The 1984 Convention adopted criteria for evaluating federal tax policies as a League position and a two-year study of U.S. fiscal policy. The three-part study focused on tax policy, deficit issues and entitlement funding. League members completed the tax policy portion of the study in time to position the League as a major force in the tax reform movement of 1985-1986. As Congress debated major legislation to broaden the income tax base, the League became a recognized leader in pushing for passage of reform legislation. The League achieved a major victory after mobilizing League members and activists to urge members of Congress to pass broad-based, fair and progressive legislation. As part of its strong legislative campaign, the League opposed a value-added tax as regressive. The League supported taxing capital gains as ordinary income and urged the removal of loopholes in the tax law.

The final two stages of the study, concluded in 1986, gave the League new tools for responding to federal deficit and budget issues. Under the deficit position, the League has supported selective cuts in defense spending that target military investment rather than readiness, in accord with the LWVUS Military Policy and Defense Spending position.

In determining what national security crises might call for deficit spending, the League is guided by its International Relations positions, including U.S. Relations with Developing Countries. The League also can, if necessary, support selective cuts in nondefense discretionary spending. In determining its stance, the LWVUS will be guided by its Social Policy, Natural Resources, Representative Government and International Relations positions and priorities.

As Congress continued in 1986 to grapple with extraordinary federal deficits and budget dilemmas, the League took a comprehensive approach to the budget battle that combined support for increased funding for human needs, for selective cuts in defense spending and for necessary revenue increases. The deficit position enabled the League to oppose a balanced budget constitutional amendment in March 1986.

The deficit position, like the tax policy position, applies only at the federal level. Thus, LWVUS opposition to the line-item veto and to a constitutionally mandated balanced budget applies only to the federal government. Under the LWVUS deficit position, state Leagues will be expected to oppose state legislative resolutions and other actions calling for a constitutional amendment requiring a balanced budget.

Since the state budgeting process occurs under different constitutional arrangements and laws, the conclusions of the federal deficit study do not overrule any current state League positions on state budgeting processes, nor can they be used at the state level without separate state League study and member agreement on the subjects.

The Funding of Entitlements position enables the LWVUS to support efforts to expand participation in the Social Security system (including participation by state and local government employees and other excluded groups). The League is opposed to measures that allow individuals to opt out of the system or measures to substitute private programs. The League opposes reducing Social Security benefits to achieve deficit reduction.

In 1990, the LWVUS urged the President and Congress to produce actual deficit reductions rather than masking the problem, and prodded them to rely primarily on reductions in defense spending and increased revenues through progressive taxes. In 1992, the LWVUS urged the President and Congress to address the recession and promote economic development. The League called for tax and budget reform and for rebuilding the nation's infrastructure.

As the federal deficit grew, the "balanced-budget" amendment to the Constitution was introduced in Congress as a political expedient to control the federal budget. The League successfully fought against passage in the House in 1992 and both houses in 1994. The League argued it would dangerously upset the federal balance of powers and hurt the economy.

In 1995, the federal deficit began to shrink, but the push for a constitutional amendment to require a balanced budget grew. The League lobbied and brought grassroots pressure to oppose this dangerous and misleading proposal, arguing that it would hamstring the government's ability to stimulate the economy in time of recession and to respond to natural disasters. Amendment opponents prevailed then and in 1996-97. League grassroots pressure was key in defeating balanced budget Constitutional amendment efforts.

In December 1998, the League and others signed a letter urging President Clinton to use the budget surplus to invest in programs that benefit the American people, including education, health care, human needs and the environment.

In 1999, when debate over Social Security's future heated up with various proposals to "privatize" the Social Security system, the LWVUS endorsed the principles of the New Century Alliance for Social Security, emphasizing Social Security's central role in family income protection. The League's stance is based on support for a federal role in providing mandatory, universal, old-age, survivors, disability and health insurance.

In the 108th Congress, the League joined with several hundred other organizations, lobbying against tax cut legislation because it was fundamentally unfair and jeopardized the nation's ability to meet its domestic and foreign responsibilities.

Responding to Congressional efforts to cut funding to the poorest of Americans during the 112th and 113th Congresses, the League lobbied in support of principles and programs that benefit low income Americans while opposing tax breaks for the wealthiest in the country.

THE LEAGUE'S POSITION

The League of Women Voters believes federal fiscal policy should provide for:

- **Adequate and flexible funding of federal government programs through an equitable tax system that is progressive overall and that relies primarily on a broad-based income tax**
- **Responsible deficit policies**
- **A federal role in providing mandatory, universal, old-age, survivors, disability and health insurance.**

TAX POLICY

The League of Women Voters believes the federal tax system should:

- **Be fair and equitable**
- **Provide adequate resources for government programs while allowing flexibility for financing future program changes**
- **Be understandable to the taxpayer and encourage compliance**
- **Accomplish its objectives without creating undue administrative problems.**

The League of Women Voters believes that the federal tax system, taken as a whole, should be progressive, not proportional.

The League supports income as the major tax base for federal revenues; believes that the federal income tax should be broad-based with minimal tax preferences and a progressive rate structure; opposes a value-added tax or a national sales tax in the federal revenue system.

Statement of Position on Fiscal Policy, as Adopted by 1984 Convention and as Announced by National Board, March 1985, January 1986 and June 1986.

FURTHER GUIDELINES

Under this position, the League of Women Voters would support tax measures that broaden the base and improve the equity of the income tax while working to incorporate progressivity into the tax system, taken as a whole.

In evaluating specific tax preferences, the League will use the following criteria:

- Whether the tax preference promotes equity and progressivity
- Whether the tax preference effectively furthers League of Women Voters program goals
- Whether the tax preference is the most efficient means of achieving its purpose
- Whether the revenue loss from the tax preference is justifiable

FEDERAL DEFICIT

The League of Women Voters believes that the current federal deficit should be reduced. In order to reduce the deficit, the government should rely primarily on reductions in defense spending through selective cuts and on increased revenue through a tax system that is broad-based with progressive rates. The government also should achieve whatever savings possible through improved efficiency and management. The League opposes across-the-board federal spending cuts.

The League recognizes that deficit spending is sometimes appropriate and therefore opposes a constitutionally mandated balanced budget for the federal government. The League could support deficit spending, if necessary, for stimulating the economy during recession and depression, meeting social needs in times of high unemployment and meeting defense needs in times of national security crises. The League opposes a federal budget line-item veto.

FUNDING OF ENTITLEMENTS

The League of Women Voters believes that the federal government has a role in funding and providing for old-age, survivors, disability and health insurance. For such insurance programs, participation should be mandatory and coverage should be universal. Federal deficit reduction should not be achieved by reducing Social Security benefits.

HEALTH CARE

In 1990, the LWVUS undertook a two-year study of the funding and delivery of health care in the United States. Phase 1 studied the delivery and policy goals of the U.S. health care system; Phase 2 focused on health care financing and administration. The LWVUS announced its initial health care position in April 1992 and the final position in April 1993.

The health care position outlines the goals the LWVUS believes are fundamental for U.S. health care policy. These include policies that promote access to a basic level of quality care at an affordable cost for all U.S. residents and strong cost-control mechanisms to ensure the efficient and economical delivery of care. The Meeting Basic Human Needs position also addresses access to health care.

The health care position enumerates services League members believe are of highest priority for a basic level of quality care: the prevention of disease, health promotion and education, primary care (including prenatal and reproductive health care), acute care, long-term care and mental health care. Dental, vision and hearing care are recognized as important services but of lower priority when measured against the added cost involved. Comments from numerous state and local Leagues, however, emphasized that these services are essential for children.

To achieve more equitable distribution of services, the League endorses increasing the availability of resources in medically underserved areas, training providers in needed fields of care, standardizing the services provided under publicly funded health care programs and insurance reforms.

The LWVUS health care position includes support for strong mechanisms to contain rising health care costs. Particular methods to promote the efficient and economical delivery of care in the United States include regional planning for the allocation of resources, reducing administrative costs, reforming the malpractice system, copayments and deductibles, and managed care. In accordance with the position's call for health care at an affordable cost, copayments and deductibles are acceptable cost containment mechanisms only if they are based on an individual's ability to pay. In addition, cost containment mechanisms should not interfere with the delivery of quality health care.

The position calls for a national health insurance plan financed through general taxes, commonly known as the "single-payer" approach. The position also supports an employer-based system that provides universal access to health care as an important step toward a national health insurance plan. The League opposes a strictly private market-based model of financing the health care system. With regard to administration of the U.S. health care system, the League supports a combination of private and public sectors or a combination of federal, state and/or regional agencies. The League supports a general income tax increase to finance national health care reform.

The League strongly believes that should the allocation of resources become necessary to reform the U.S. health care system, the ability of a patient to pay for services should not be a consideration. In determining how health care resources should be allocated, the League emphasizes the consideration of the following factors, taken together: the urgency of the medical condition, the life expectancy of the patient, the expected outcome of the treatment, the cost of the procedure, the duration of care, the quality of life of the patient after the treatment, and the wishes of the patient and the family.

As the LWVUS was completing Phase 2 of the study, the issue of health care reform was rising to the top of the country's legislative agenda. In April 1993, as soon as the study results were announced, the LWVUS met with White House Health Care officials to present the results of the League's position. Since then, the League has actively participated in the health care debate.

The LWVUS testified in fall 1993 before the House Ways and Means Subcommittee on Health, the Energy and Commerce Committee and the Education and Labor Committee, calling for comprehensive health care reform based on the League position. The League joined two coalitions—one comprised of consumer, business, labor, provider and senior groups working for comprehensive health care reform, and the other comprised of groups supporting the single-payer approach to health care reform.

Throughout 1994, the League actively lobbied in support of comprehensive reform, including universal coverage, cost containment, single-payer or employer mandate and a strong benefits package. The League emphasized LWVUS support for the inclusion of reproductive health care, including abortion, in any health benefits package.

The LWVEF initiated community education efforts on health care issues with the Understanding Health Care Policy project in the early 1990s. The project provided training and resources for Leagues to conduct broad-based community outreach and education on health care policy issues with the goal of expanding community participation in the debate.

In spring 1994, the LWVEF and the Kaiser Family Foundation (KFF) undertook a major citizen education effort, Citizen's Voice for Citizen's Choice: A Campaign for a Public Voice on Health Care Reform. The project delivered objective information on health care reform to millions of Americans across the country through local and state Leagues sponsored town meetings in major media markets nationwide, involving members of Congress and other leading policy makers and analysts in health care discussions with citizens. In September 1994, the LWVEF and KFF held a National Satellite Town Meeting on Health Care Reform, with 200+ downlink sites across the country. They also undertook a major television advertising promotion of public participation in the health care debate.

In 1997, the LWVUS joined 100 national, state and local organizations in successfully urging Congress to pass strong bipartisan child health care legislation. In 1998, the LWVUS began working for a Patients' Bill of Rights, aimed at giving Americans participating in managed care health plans greater access to specialists without going through a gatekeeper, the right to emergency room care using the "reasonably prudent person" standard, a speedy appeals process when there is a dispute with insurers and other rights.

In 1998, the LWVEF again partnered with KFF and state and local Leagues on a citizen education project, this time focused on Medicare reform, patients' bill of rights and other health care issues. In the first phase, more than 6,500 citizens participated in focus groups, community dialogues and public meetings. Their views were reflected in "How Americans Talk about Medicare Reform: The Public Voice," presented to the National Bipartisan Commission on the Future of Medicare in March 1999. The report emphasized that people value Medicare but recognize its flaws. Fairness, responsibility, efficiency and access were identified as important values for any reforms of the Medicare system.

In spring 2000, the LWVEF and KFF developed and distributed two guides, *Join the Debate: Your Guide to Health Issues in the 2000 Election* and *A Leader's Handbook for Holding Community Dialogues*. The project focused on five issues under debate in the election: the uninsured, managed care and patients' rights, Medicare reform, prescription drug coverage and long-term care.

In the late 90s, the LWVUS lobbied in support of a strong Patients' Bill of Rights. Despite close votes in 2000, Senate opponents continued to block passage. At Convention 2000, League delegates lobbied their members of Congress to pass a strong, comprehensive Patients' Bill of Rights, but it was shelved as Election 2000 drew near.

In the 108th Congress, the League lobbied in support of the Health Care Access Resolution. In 2003, the League opposed the Medicare Prescription Drug bill, which the President signed into law, because of provisions that undermined universal coverage in Medicare.

In May 2006, the League urged Senators to oppose the Health Insurance Marketplace Modernization and Affordability Act (HIMMA), which purported to expand healthcare coverage, while actually limiting critical consumer protections provided in many states.

From 2007-2009, the League urged reauthorization of the State Children's Health Insurance Program (SCHIP), which provided health care coverage in 2007 to six million low-income children; the efforts were rewarded with reauthorization in early 2009.

In 2010, two decades of League work to ensure access to affordable, quality health care for all Americans and protect patients' rights celebrated success when the Affordable Care Act (ACA) was signed into law. The League remains vigilant in light of current efforts to repeal or diminish the law in Congress and the courts.

In the 112th Congress, the League continued to fight attempts to repeal the Affordable Care Act and to limit provisions that provide health and reproductive services for women. State Leagues began to work with their legislatures to implement the ACA and the LWVUS signed on to an *amicus* brief in the challenge to the Affordable Care Act, which was upheld by the Supreme Court.

In 2013, as opposition to the ACA was raised in the legislative, regulatory and judicial processes, the LWVUS submitted comments opposing religious exemptions for contraceptive services. This debate continued in the courts and the League joined with other concerned organizations in opposing broad "religious exemptions" to the requirement that all insurance plans provide access to contraception as basic care in the 2014 Supreme Court case of *Burwell v. Hobby Lobby Stores.*

Judicial action continued in 2015 as supporters, including the League, submitted an *amicus* brief in the case of *Burwell v. King,* which challenged the availability of tax subsidies for people who purchase health insurance on a marketplace administered by the federal government. The ACA gave states a choice not to administer its own marketplace. The brief outlined how tax subsidies are essential to women's health and critical to the ACA's continued viability.

The League continued to support implementation of the ACA at the state level and expansion of the Medicaid program, as provided by the ACA. The League also continued its strong support for continued funding of the Children's Health Insurance Program (CHIP).

THE LEAGUE'S POSITION
The League of Women Voters believes that a basic level of quality health care at an affordable cost should be available to all U.S. residents. Other U.S. health care policy goals should include the equitable distribution of services, efficient and economical delivery of care, advancement of medical research and technology, and a reasonable total national expenditure level for health care.

BASIC LEVEL OF QUALITY CARE
Every U.S. resident should have access to a basic level of care that includes:

- **The prevention of disease**
- **Health promotion and education**
- **Primary care (including prenatal and reproductive health)**
- **Acute care**
- **Long-term care**
- **Mental health care**

Every U.S. resident should have access to affordable, quality in- and out-patient behavioral health care, including needed medications and supportive service that is integrated with, and achieves parity with, physical health care.

Dental, vision and hearing care also are important but lower in priority. The League believes that under any system of health care reform, consumers/patients should be permitted to purchase services or insurance coverage beyond the basic level.

FINANCING AND ADMINISTRATION
The League favors a national health insurance plan financed through general taxes in place of individual insurance premiums. As the United States moves toward a national health insurance plan, an employer-based system of health care reform that provides universal access is acceptable to the League. The League supports administration of the U.S. health care system either by a combination of the private and public sectors or by a combination of federal, state and/or regional government agencies.

The League is opposed to a strictly private market-based model of financing the health care system. The League also is opposed to the administration of the health care system solely by the private sector or the states.

TAXES

The League supports increased taxes to finance a basic level of health care for all U.S. residents, provided health care reforms contain effective cost control strategies.

COST CONTROL

The League believes that efficient and economical delivery of care can be enhanced by such cost control methods as:

- The reduction of administrative costs
- Regional planning for the allocation of personnel, facilities and equipment
- The establishment of maximum levels of public reimbursement to providers
- Malpractice reform
- The use of managed care
- Utilization review of treatment
- Mandatory second opinions before surgery or extensive treatment
- Consumer accountability through deductibles and copayments

EQUITY ISSUES

The League believes that health care services could be more equitably distributed by:

- Allocating medical resources to underserved areas
- Providing for training health care professionals in needed fields of care
- Standardizing basic levels of service for publicly funded health care programs
- Requiring insurance plans to use community rating instead of experience rating
- Establishing insurance pools for small businesses and organizations

ALLOCATION OF RESOURCES TO INDIVIDUALS

The League believes that the ability of a patient to pay for services should not be a consideration in the allocation of health care resources. Limited resources should

be allocated based on the following criteria considered together:

- The urgency of the medical condition
- The life expectancy of the patient
- The expected outcome of the treatment
- The cost of the procedure
- The duration of care
- The wishes of the patient and the family

BEHAVIORAL HEALTH

The League of Women Voters supports:

- Behavioral Health as the nationally accepted term that includes both mental illness and substance use disorder
- Access for all people to affordable, quality in- and out-patient behavioral health care, including needed medications and supportive services
- Behavioral Health care that is integrated with, and achieves parity with, physical health care
- Early and affordable behavioral health diagnosis and treatment for children and youth from early childhood through adolescence
- Early and appropriate diagnosis and treatment for children and adolescents that is family-focused and community-based
- Access to safe and stable housing for people with behavioral health challenges, including those who are chronically homeless
- Effective re-entry planning and follow-up for people released from both behavioral health hospitalization and the criminal justice system
- Problem solving or specialty courts, including mental health and drug courts, in all judicial districts to provide needed treatment and avoid inappropriate entry into the criminal justice system
- Health education from early childhood throughout life that integrates all aspects of social, emotional and physical health and wellness
- Efforts to decrease the stigmatization of, and normalize, behavioral health problems and care

Statement of Position on Health Care, as Announced by National Board, April 1993 and supplemented by concurrence, June 2016.

IMMIGRATION

In the 111th Congress, the League lobbied in support of the DREAM (Development, Relief and Education for Alien Minors) Act that would provide a path to citizenship for young immigrants who complete a college degree or serve in the military, thereby enabling them to be a fully productive part of American society. The legislation passed the House, but lacked enough votes to overcome a filibuster in the Senate.

THE LEAGUE'S POSITION

The League of Women Voters believes that immigration policies should promote reunification of immediate families; meet the economic, business and employment needs of the United States; and be responsive to those facing political persecution or humanitarian crises. Provision should also be made for qualified persons to enter the United States on student visas. All persons should receive fair treatment under the law.

The League supports federal immigration law that provides an efficient, expeditious system (with minimal or no backlogs) for legal entry of immigrants into the United States.

To complement these goals the League supports federal policies to improve economies, education, job opportunities and living conditions in nations with large emigrating populations.

In transition to a reformed system, the League supports provisions for unauthorized immigrants already in the country to earn legal status

The League supports federal payments to impacted communities to address the financial costs borne by states and local governments with large immigrant populations.

CRITERIA FOR LEGAL ADMISSION TO THE UNITED STATES

The League supports the following criteria for legal admission of persons into the United States:

- Family reunification of spouses or minor children with authorized immigrants or citizens
- Flight from persecution or response to humanitarian crises in home countries
- Economic, business and employment needs in the Unites States
- Education and training needs of the United States
- Educational program opportunities
- Lack of a history of serious criminal activity.

ADMINISTRATION AND ENFORCEMENT

The League supports due process for all persons, including the right to a fair hearing, right to counsel, right of appeal and right to humane treatment. The League supports:

- Improved technology to facilitate employer verification of employee status
- Verification documents, such as status cards and work permits, with secure identifiers
- Significant fines and penalties for employers who hire unauthorized workers
- Improved technology for sharing information among federal agencies
- More effective tracking of individuals who enter the United States
- Increased personnel at borders.

The League also supports programs allowing foreign workers to enter and leave the United States to meet seasonal or sporadic labor needs.

UNAUTHORIZED IMMIGRANTS ALREADY IN THE UNITED STATES

In achieving overall policy goals, the League supports a system for unauthorized immigrants already in the country to earn legal status, including citizenship, by paying taxes, learning English, studying civics and meeting other relevant criteria. While policy reforms, including a path to legal status, remain unachieved, the

League does not support deporting unauthorized immigrants who have no history of criminal activity.

Statement of Position on Immigration, as Announced by National Board, April 2008.

MEETING BASIC HUMAN NEEDS

After adopting the Meeting Basic Human Needs position in 1988, the League reorganized the Social Policy program in 1990. This reorganization combined several existing positions to address the basic needs of all people for food, shelter, and access to health care and transportation. The Meeting Basic Human Needs position encompasses previous positions on income assistance and transportation. The issue of housing supply was separated from the fair housing position, which is still under Equality of Opportunity, and put under the Meeting Basic Human Needs position.

Income Assistance

The 1970 Convention adopted a study of alternatives to welfare. As a result of the study, members agreed to support a system of federalized income assistance. The position, adopted in 1971, suggests criteria for such a system and for minimum uniform standards of eligibility for both cash benefits and supportive services (in-kind benefits). The position is closely linked with the Employment position in encouraging work and in emphasizing the responsibility of the federal government to help those who cannot find work, those whose earnings are insufficient to meet basic needs or those who are unable to work.

Adoption of the position coincided with a congressional effort to make major changes in the welfare system in 1971-72. The League mounted an all-out lobbying effort in support of the legislation, despite recognized its shortcomings. In the late 1970s, the League attempted unsuccessfully to strengthen a number of federal welfare reform proposals. The League has supported a variety of specific programs for income assistance and in-kind benefits such as food stamps, low-income energy assistance, child-care legislation, reform of unemployment compensation and Aid to Families with Dependent Children programs, and housing subsidies. Comprehensive child care remains an elusive but critically needed support service for women seeking employment. In each case the League has pressed for: uniform minimum federal standards of eligibility, uniform standards for benefits based on need and standards for quality of services.

Support Services

The League has opposed cutoffs of Medicaid funding for abortion as violating the supportive services provisions of the Income Assistance position and because such actions clearly discriminate against economically disadvantaged women.

In the 1980s, national League action on income assistance focused primarily on opposition to funding cutbacks, dilution of the federal role, and changes in eligibility requirements for income maintenance programs and support services.

In 1986-88, the League worked in support of welfare reform legislation in Congress, culminating in passage of the Family Support Act of 1988. The League had supported the House version, the Family Welfare Reform Act, which included provisions for education, training and employment of welfare recipients. The final bill followed the Senate version, the Family Security Act, which the League opposed. The League joined the national Coalition on Human Needs in opposing the final bill, citing inadequate funding and mandatory participation quotas. Since passage of the Act, states continue to face implementation decisions.

The League lobbied successfully in support of the Family and Medical Leave Act, designed to guarantee workers unpaid leave for illness or the birth or adoption of a child. Through the years, the League has supported the Earned Income Tax Credit as a necessary form of income assistance.

Other League efforts include lobbying Congress in 1991 and 1992 to pass the Mickey Leland Hunger Relief Act and the Freedom from Want Act, bills designed to alleviate hunger in the United States. In 1988-1990, the LWVEF coordinated an 18-month Hunger Advocacy Project designed to help state and local Leagues develop and carry out model, targeted activities to document or alleviate hunger. A guide, *Fighting Hunger in Your Community*, provided information on replicating such activities.

In 1989-1990, the LWVEF promoted discussion of a Ford Foundation report on social welfare, *The Common Good*. Three regional workshops were held on issues raised in the report, and local Leagues conducted related community education activities.

The League actively opposed welfare reform legislation proposed in the 104th Congress. During summer 1996, the White House and Congress agreed on legislation to essentially hand over welfare to the states. Despite the League's strong lobbying effort with a particular focus on the President, the bill was passed and signed into law in August 1996. State Leagues across the country monitored the implementation and effects of "reform" efforts at the state level to ensure that the benefits were provided where needed and that recipients' civil rights were protected.

In fall 2005, the League responded to the Hurricane Katrina disaster, urging Congress to protect basic human needs of those affected by securing the basics of jobs, income when work is not available, health care, food, education, child care, and housing, while also protecting and expanding the capacity of the federal government to respond by preserving and increasing funding for vital services and not sapping revenues through misdirected tax cuts.

As the 113th Congress cut funding and changed eligibility formulas for SNAP (Supplemental Nutrition Assistance Program, formerly the Food Stamp program), the League joined with other organizations to urge Congress to strengthen, not weaken the program.

Housing Supply

During the late 1960s and early 1970s, the League worked for a number of federal housing programs. In 1974, League support was channeled into aspects of the Housing and Community Development Act, which consolidated federal assistance under a block grant approach. The League fought against congressional action to weaken the Community Development Block Grant program through drastic cuts in the full range of authorized low- and moderate-income subsidies for both rehabilitation and new housing.

Throughout the 1980s, the League continued to support increased funding to add to and maintain the existing stock of federally assisted housing for very low-income persons. LWVUS efforts included working as a member of the National Low Income Housing Coalition to urge passage of 1987 legislation authorizing HUD's low-income housing and community development programs, as well as endorsing the 1989 Housing Now march on Washington.

As a member of the Low Income Housing Coalition's Women and Housing Task Force, the LWVUS endorsed recommendations predicated on the conviction that every person and family should have decent, safe and affordable housing. State and local Leagues have worked to increase the supply of low and moderate-income housing through efforts to change zoning laws and to set up shared housing services.

In 2002, the LWVUS formally endorsed legislation to establish the National Housing Trust Fund which uses surplus funds from the Federal Housing Administration (FHA) to create new housing for low-income families.

Transportation

LWVUS concern about public transportation grew out of efforts on behalf of equal opportunity for employment and housing. The 1971 Air Quality position added another dimension to this concern by urging "measures to reduce vehicular pollution and development of alternate transportation systems." In 1972, the LWVUS Board responded to questions of interpretation by synthesizing the two positions into a unified Transportation position. In 1976, following League concurrence on the Energy Conservation position, the LWVUS Board reaffirmed the national League's Transportation position. In 1979, the Urban Policy position reinforced the theme that federal aid for highway construction should be reduced; the Transportation position language was revised to make that point clear.

The League first put the position to work by backing a national coalition's efforts to amend the Federal Aid Highway Act of 1972 to permit financing part of the costs of urban mass transit from highway trust funds. The League also supported the National Mass Transportation Assistance Act of 1974. Later the focus shifted to prevent stalling or cutting of federal assistance to mass transit systems.

In response to the urgency to improve and promote public transportation systems, the 1980 Convention voted to give greater emphasis to the Transportation position. In 1988, it was incorporated into the Meeting Basic Human Needs position. Leagues continue to use the Transportation position with their own local or ILO positions to back local and regional moves to improve mass transit and support other alternatives, such as express lanes for buses and carpools.

THE LEAGUE'S POSITION

The League of Women Voters believes that one of the goals of social policy in the United States should be to promote self-sufficiency for individuals and families and that the most effective social programs are those designed to prevent or reduce poverty.

Persons who are unable to work, whose earnings are inadequate or for whom jobs are not available have the right to an income and/or services sufficient to meet their basic needs for food, shelter and access to health care.

The federal government should set minimum, uniform standards and guidelines for social welfare programs and should bear primary responsibility for financing programs designed to help meet the basic needs of individuals and families. State and local governments, as well as the private sector, should have a secondary role in financing food, housing and health care programs. Income assistance programs should be financed primarily by the federal government with state governments assuming secondary responsibility.

PREVENTING AND REDUCING POVERTY

In order to prevent or reduce poverty, the LWVUS supports policies and programs designed to:

- **Increase job opportunities**
- **Increase access to health insurance**
- **Provide support services such as child care and transportation**
- **Provide opportunities and/or incentives for basic or remedial education and job training**
- **Decrease teen pregnancy; ensure that noncustodial parents contribute to the support of their children.**

ACCESS TO HEALTH CARE

The League believes access to health care includes the following:

- **Preventive care**
- **Primary care**
- **Maternal and child health care**
- **Emergency care, catastrophic care**
- **Nursing home care and mental health care as well as access to substance abuse programs**
- **Health and sex education programs**
- **Nutrition programs.**

ACCESS TO TRANSPORTATION

The League believes that energy-efficient and environmentally sound transportation systems should afford better access to housing and jobs and the League will continue to examine transportation policies in light of these goals.

Statement of Position on Meeting Basic Human Needs, as Revised by the National Board, January 1989, based on positions reached from 1971 through 1988.

FURTHER GUIDELINES AND CRITERIA

CRITERIA FOR INCOME ASSISTANCE

- Eligibility of all low-income individuals for assistance should be based on need. Eligibility should be established through simplified procedures such as a declaration of need, spot-checked in a manner similar to that used in checking the validity of income tax returns.

- Benefit levels should be sufficient to provide decent, adequate standards for food, clothing and shelter. Minimum income standards should be adjusted for regional differences in the cost of living and should be revised periodically to take into account changes in the purchasing value of the dollar. Until a federal welfare program achieves an adequate level of benefits, some states will need to supplement federal payments.
- There should be increasing emphasis on cash assistance, but in-kind assistance (e.g., food stamps, housing subsidies, medical aid) should be continued to help assure that these needs are met.
- Under a revised program participants should not have their benefits reduced.
- Privacy of participants should be protected. All administrative procedures should be conducted with respect for the rights and dignity of the individuals.
- Work should be encouraged. Participants' total income should increase as earnings increase. Counseling, realistic training for actual jobs and financial incentives should be the links between job programs and income assistance.

CRITERIA FOR SUPPORTIVE SERVICES

- Supportive services should be available but not compulsory for participants in income assistance programs. Most important among these are child care, counseling, transportation, and family planning, health care and legal services.
- Fees for supportive services should be based on ability to pay and be free where necessary.
- Facilities and services for participants should be the same as for the general public.
- The federal government should exert leadership in setting standards for eligibility, for the quality of services and for adequate funding.
- Participants in the programs should be included in program development and implementation, and the administration of social services programs should be responsive to the needs of the people being served.

- Wherever possible, these services should be conveniently located in the neighborhood.
- Transportation systems should afford better access to housing and jobs and should also provide energy efficient and environmentally sound transportation.
- Government programs that require recipients of assistance to engage in work-related programs would be acceptable only if the following protections are guaranteed to the participants:
  o Job training
  o Basic education
  o Exemptions for primary care givers
  o Supplemental support services such as child care and transportation
  o Equitable compensation to ensure that program participants earn the same wages and benefits as other employees performing similar work
  o A disregard of some earned income for purposes of calculating benefit levels.

CRITERIA FOR HOUSING SUPPLY

The following considerations can be applied to programs and policies to provide a decent home and a suitable living environment for every American family:

- The responsibility for achieving national housing goals rests primarily with the federal government, which should:
  o Assure that our economic system is functioning to produce and maintain sufficient decent housing for citizens at all income levels
  o Compensate for any failure or inadequacy of the system by building, financing, renting and selling homes to those citizens whose housing needs are not being met
  o Give a variety of incentives to local jurisdictions to encourage them to provide within their boundaries an adequate supply of decent housing for low- and moderate-income groups
  o Withhold federal funds from communities that fail to encourage such housing.
- State and local governments should assist by establishing effective agencies to aid, promote, coordinate and supplement the housing programs of the federal government and the private sector.

93

- Government at all levels must make available sufficient funds for housing-assistance programs.
- When families or individuals cannot afford decent housing, government should provide assistance in the form of income and/or subsidized housing.
- Government programs providing subsidies to the building, financing and insuring industries for housing for lower-income families should be evaluated in terms of units produced rather than in terms of benefits accruing to these industries.
- Government at all levels should develop policies that will assure sufficient land at reasonable cost on which to develop housing and that will assure fulfillment of other goals such as access to employment, preservation of open space, environmental cleanliness and beauty, and other aspects of a suitable living environment.
- Regional and metropolitan planning should be promoted to prevent haphazard urban growth, and housing for low- and moderate-income families should be provided as a part of all planned neighborhoods or communities.
- Lower-income families should not be segregated in large developments or neighborhoods. As their economic status improves, lower-income families should be enabled to continue to live in the same units as private tenants or as homeowners, if they are so inclined.
- Housing should be designed to meet human needs and should be built with amenities that will encourage economic integration within apartment buildings as well as within neighborhoods.
- Publicly assisted housing should be included in viable, balanced communities, with provision for quality public services and facilities, including schools, transportation, recreation, etc., that will encourage integration and stability.
- Zoning practices and procedures that will counteract racial and economic isolation should be promoted.
- State and local governments should adopt and enforce:
  - Uniform building codes with standards based on performance
  - Housing codes to protect the health and safety of all citizens.

- State and local tax structures should be examined and revised to:
  - Benefit communities that build housing for lower-income families
  - Encourage private owners to improve their homes
  - Reduce speculative land costs.
- Government, industry and labor should encourage innovative building techniques to reduce the cost of housing production.
- Rights of tenants to negotiate for proper maintenance, management of facilities and services should be protected.
- Housing programs should be administered by individuals trained for the jobs and sympathetic with the needs of their clientele.
- Citizen groups should participate in the development of publicly assisted housing programs by:
  - Evaluating performance
  - Activating nonprofit sponsorships
  - Supporting legislation
  - Developing public awareness of housing discrimination and need.

CHILD CARE

The League has long recognized that child-care programs are a key supportive service for poor families.

The 1988 LWVUS Convention adopted child care as a priority and separated the child care position within the Social Policy position. The League supported a compromise child-care bill, signed by the President in 1990, which provided financial assistance to low-income families for child care; increased the availability of child care through resource and referral programs and training for child-care workers; and required states to establish health and safety standards for day care. Then Leagues across the country monitored and commented on the regulatory process as the Department of Health and Human Services wrote implementing regulations.

LWVEF activities included a 1990-1991 School-Age Child Care Project. The goal was to help local Leagues serve as catalysts in targeted communities to increase the availability of affordable, quality school-age child care for low- and moderate-income families. In 1992, the LWVEF published a community action guide using the model League projects to help other communities implement similar programs.

In summer 1998, the LWVUS and other groups urged congressional action on child care and the passage of a substantial increase in guaranteed funds for the Child Care Development Block Grant.

In early 2002, the League joined other groups in support of legislation to reauthorize the Temporary Assistance to Needy Families program (TANF) and provide for comprehensive reforms to help those on welfare become self-sufficient. It was not adopted.

THE LEAGUE'S POSITION
The League of Women Voters support programs, services and policies at all levels of government to expand the supply of affordable, quality child care for all who need it, in order to increase access to employment and to prevent and reduce poverty.

Statement of Position on Child Care, as Adopted by the 1988 Convention, based on positions reached from 1969 through 1988.

EARLY INTERVENTION FOR CHILDREN AT RISK

The position on Early Intervention for Children at Risk was adopted by concurrence at Convention 1994; it was based on state and local League work.

In 1995, the LWVEF published a comprehensive kit, designed to help Leagues and other groups advocate and work for children in their communities. In June 1996, the League endorsed the Stand for Children, a national day of commitment to improving the lives of children throughout the country.

THE LEAGUE'S POSITION
The League of Women Voters believes that early intervention and prevention measures are effective in helping children reach their full potential. The League supports policies and programs at all levels of the community and government that promote the well-being, encourage the full development and ensure the safety of all children. These include:

- **Child abuse/neglect prevention**
- **Teen pregnancy prevention**
- **Quality health care, including nutrition and prenatal care**
- **Early childhood education**
- **Developmental services, emphasizing children ages 0-3**
- **Family support services**
- **Violence prevention.**

Statement of Position on Early Intervention for Children at Risk, as Adopted by the 1994 Convention.

VIOLENCE PREVENTION

The 1994 Convention adopted by concurrence a position on Violence Prevention, based on state and local League work. The League subsequently endorsed the Violence Against Women Act, which Congress passed and the President signed in 1994 as part of a comprehensive crime bill.

THE LEAGUE'S POSITION
The League of Women Voters supports violence prevention programs in all communities and action to support:

- **Public and private development and coordination of programs that emphasize the primary prevention of violence**
- **The active role of government and social institutions in preventing violent behavior**
- **The allocation of public monies in government programs to prevent violence.**

Statement of Position on Violence Prevention, as Adopted by the 1994 Convention.

GUN CONTROL

The 1990 Convention took the then rare step of adopting the gun control position by concurrence. Proponents had sent two informational mailings to all Leagues before Convention. Spirited debate on the Convention floor persuaded the Convention to concur with the statement proposed by the LWV of Illinois.

Following the Convention action, the LWVUS wrote to all members of Congress, announcing the League's new position on gun control and urging passage of federal legislation to control the proliferation of handguns and semi-automatic assault weapons in the United States. In 1991, the League joined with other organizations to support legislation banning semi-automatic assault weapons. In 1992 and 1993, the League supported congressional passage of the Brady bill, to institute a five-day waiting period and background check for the purchase of handguns. Following enactment of the Brady bill in November 1993, the League stepped up its efforts in a successful 1994 House campaign to force inclusion of the assault weapons ban in the final conference report on omnibus crime legislation.

Addressing constitutional arguments affecting gun control, the 1994 Convention voted to amend the position on gun control based on federal court decisions limiting the meaning of the Second Amendment's "right to keep and bear arms." This section of the position was nullified by the Supreme Court decisions in *District of Columbia v. Heller, 2008* and *McDonald v. Chicago, 2010.*

Throughout 1995-1996, opponents of the assault weapons ban and Brady bill pushed for repeal, but the League and others convinced Congress otherwise.

The 1998 Convention again amended the position with: "The League supports regulating firearms for consumer safety."

The 106th Congress defeated LWVUS-supported gun control measures to close major loopholes in the law: mandating background checks for all gun show purchases and child safety locks on guns.

The LWVUS endorsed and League members joined the Mother's Day 2000 Million Mom March that demonstrated citizens' call for common-sense gun control measures.

In 2004, the League voiced strong concern over the Protection of Lawful Commerce in Arms Act, which would grant special protection for the gun industry by barring city, county or individual lawsuits against gun manufacturers and dismiss pending cases

The League supported legislation to extend the Assault Weapons Ban, which expired in September 2004. The LWVUS also supported language to close the Gun Show Loophole to require all dealers to run criminal background checks at gun shows.

In the 2000s, the League opposed congressional attempts to repeal District of Columbia gun safety laws because such action interfered with the right of self-government for DC citizens.

THE LEAGUE'S POSITION
The League of Women Voters believes that the proliferation of handguns and semi-automatic assault weapons in the United States is a major health and safety threat to its citizens. The League supports strong federal measures to limit the accessibility and regulate the ownership of these weapons by private citizens. The League supports regulating firearms for consumer safety.

The League supports licensing procedures for gun ownership by private citizens to include a waiting period for background checks, personal identity verification, gun safety education and annual license renewal. The license fee should be adequate to bear the cost of education and verification.

The League supports a ban on "Saturday night specials," enforcement of strict penalties for the improper possession of and crimes committed with handguns and assault weapons, and allocation of resources to better regulate and monitor gun dealers.

Statement of Position on Gun Control, as Adopted by 1990 Convention and amended by the 1994 and 1998 Conventions.

URBAN POLICY

Recognizing that the League's program already had many urban implications, the 1976 Convention added Cities/Urban Crisis to the national program as a "specific focus for information and action on urban problems." Members examined urban connections among existing League positions in order to open up new action opportunities to address the desperate plight of many urban areas.

The 1978 Convention reaffirmed the League's interest in the urban problem by adopting an "evaluation of urban policy options, with emphasis on fiscal policy." Leagues drew on their preliminary explorations of urban problems for a more structured study of the appropriate federal role in the intergovernmental responsibility for cities. In June 1979, the national board announced a new position, enabling the League to take a strong stand on targeting federal assistance to distressed cities, especially through urban economic development assistance programs to encourage private reinvestment in cities. It also supports general and targeted direct financial assistance to cities.

During the consensus process, it was made clear that restoring economic health to the nation's cities requires combined state, local and federal government efforts. State Leagues have used the position to work for targeted state aid to distressed areas, and local Leagues have pushed for improved city management to make better use of diminishing resources.

The League's first national action campaign under the position involved the 1980 reauthorization of General Revenue Sharing. Building upon the previous monitoring and action to strengthen GRS (see Equal Access position), the Urban Policy position reaffirmed support for strong civil rights, citizen participation requirements, auditing standards, and for a more equitable distribution of funds. The League worked with a coalition toward these ends, and was successful on all but the last issue.

Under the Urban Policy position, the League supported expansion of Economic Development programs and the reauthorization of Urban Development Action Grants (UDAG). In efforts to bring more jobs to urban areas, the League also has supported the location of federal facilities in distressed cities.

Local and state Leagues implemented the position by fighting to save downtown businesses from extinction, commenting on local UDAG applications, working for public/private cooperation in the revitalization of city neighborhoods, and undertaking citizen education activities to spur interest in improving the quality of urban life.

In 1979, under a grant from the National Endowment for the Humanities, the LWVEF and a number of local Leagues worked to increase public awareness of urban problems and solutions. Another grant enabled the LWVEF to sponsor an exchange between Leagues in the industrial heartland and the Sunbelt.

The 1980 Convention changed Urban Crisis to Urban Policy. A new focus on urban transportation united the League's long-time concerns about access to jobs, air quality, land use and energy with newer concerns about urban economic development and municipal finances.

THE LEAGUE'S POSITION

The League of Women Voters believes that it is in the national interest to promote the well-being of America's cities.

Sharply targeted federal assistance to distressed cities should be central to this policy. The federal government should give highest priority in urban policy to measures that enhance the economic base of cities. The League also favors supplementary federal aid for cities in distressed fiscal condition and grants for particular program areas as strategies to counter the problems of hardship cities.

The fiscal health of cities depends on the active cooperation of all levels of government. The federal government should provide incentives to encourage states to take an active role in promoting the fiscal viability of their cities.

The League is committed to an urban environment beneficial to life and to resource management in the public interest.

Statement of Position on Urban Policy, as Announced by National Board, June 1979 and revised by the National Board in 1989.

FURTHER GUIDELINES

ECONOMIC DEVELOPMENT ASSISTANCE

The cornerstone of a national urban policy is a commitment to helping cities achieve economic strength. Federal programs to encourage private reinvestment in central cities should counter an eroding tax base and provide jobs for the inner-city unemployed. Therefore, the League supports the following federal strategies:

- Target community development programs to cities most in need
- Encourage businesses to locate or expand in distressed cities through such financial incentives as investment tax credits, loan guarantees, subsidies for hiring the long-term unemployed and interest subsidies
- Expand middle-income housing while not diminishing attention to low-income housing needs
- Target federal purchasing and location of federal facilities in distressed cities

GENERAL FINANCIAL ASSISTANCE

The League supports a variety of federal strategies, including direct general assistance, targeted to distressed cities. Such a program should include aid to counter recession. In providing federal aid for particular program areas, grants offer city governments the best opportunities to meet local needs.

In order to increase the availability of funds to city governments for capital expenditures, the federal government should use mechanisms to lower the cost of borrowing.

Aid to cities should include technical assistance to improve management capacity.

DEATH PENALTY

At Convention 2006, delegates voted to adopt a position supporting abolition of the death penalty. This decision was made in concurrence with a position adopted by the LWV of Illinois. Since that time, state Leagues have used the position to support initiatives to abolish the death penalty in their states.

THE LEAGUE'S POSITION

The League of Women Voters supports the abolition of the death penalty.

Statement of Position on Abolition of the Death Penalty, as Adopted by the 2006 Convention.

SENTENCING POLICY

At convention 2012, delegates voted to adopt a Sentencing Policy position by concurrence. The position is based on the Sentencing Policy of the LWV of the District of Columbia. In late 2013, the LWVUS supported the Smarter Sentencing Act, a Senate bill which would reduce federal sentences for non-violent drug offenders, but the bill did not come to the Senate floor.

THE LEAGUE'S POSITION
The League of Women Voters believes alternatives to imprisonment should be explored and utilized, taking into consideration the circumstances and nature of the crime. The LWVUS opposes mandatory minimum sentences for drug offenses.

Statement of Position on Sentencing Policy, as Adopted by the 2012 Convention.

HUMAN TRAFFICKING

At convention 2014, a Human Trafficking position based on the position of the League of Women Voters of New Jersey was adopted by delegates.

THE LEAGUE'S POSITION
The League of Women Voters opposes all forms of domestic and international human trafficking of adults and children, including sex trafficking and labor trafficking. We consider human trafficking to be a form of modern day slavery and believe that every measure should be taken and every effort should be made through legislation and changes in public policy to prevent human trafficking. Prosecution and penalization of traffickers and abusers should be established, and existing laws should be strictly enforced. Extensive essential services for victims should be applied where needed.

Education and awareness programs on human trafficking should be established in our communities and in our schools.

Statement of Position on Human Trafficking as adopted at the LWVUS 2014 National Convention.

PRINCIPLES

The League of Women Voters believes in representative government and in the individual liberties established in the Constitution of the United States. The League of Women Voters of the United States believes that all powers of the U.S. government should be exercised within the constitutional framework of a balance among the three branches of government: legislative, executive, and judicial.

The League of Women Voters believes that democratic government depends upon informed and active participation in government and requires that governmental bodies protect the citizen's right to know by giving adequate notice of proposed actions, holding open meetings and making public records accessible.

The League of Women Voters believes that every citizen should be protected in the right to vote; that every person should have access to free public education that provides equal opportunity for all; and that no person or group should suffer legal, economic or administrative discrimination.

The League of Women Voters believes that efficient and economical government requires competent personnel, the clear assignment of responsibility, adequate financing, and coordination among the different agencies and levels of government.

The League of Women Voters believes that responsible government should be responsive to the will of the people. Government should maintain an equitable and flexible system of taxation, promote the conservation and development of natural resources in the public interest, share in the solution of economic and social problems that affect the general welfare, promote a sound economy and adopt domestic policies that facilitate the solution of international problems.

The League of Women Voters believes that cooperation with other nations is essential in the search for solutions to world problems and that development of international organization and international law is imperative in the promotion of world peace.

WHERE DO THE PRINCIPLES COME FROM?

The Principles are "concepts of government" to which the League subscribes. They are a descendant of the Platform, which served from 1942 to 1956 as the national repository for "principles supported and positions taken by the League as a whole in fields of government to which it has given sustained attention." Since then, the Principles have served two functions, according to the LWVUS Bylaws:

- Authorization for adoption of national, state and local program (Article XII)
- A basis for taking action at the national, state and local levels (Article XII).

The appropriate Board authorizes action to implement the Principles once it determines that member understanding and agreement do exist and that action is appropriate. As with other action, when there are ramifications beyond a League's own government jurisdiction, that League should consult other Leagues affected.

The National Board suggests that any action on the Principles be taken in conjunction with current League positions to which they apply and on which member agreement and understanding are known to exist. The Principles are rather broad when standing alone, so it is necessary to exercise caution when considering using them as a basis for action. Furthermore, since 1974, most of the Principles have been an integral part of the national program, most notably in the criteria for evaluating government that appear at the end of the summary of public policy positions (page 1 above).

CPSIA information can be obtained
at www.ICGtesting.com
Printed in the USA
LVOW09s2331100418
572944LV00009BA/719/P

9 781542 787987